Contents

Making Merry at the Last Minute

Just because Christmas is a cheerful season doesn't mean things can't go wrong. For one thing, you'll almost certainly have to come up with one...or two...or 24 Christmas presents at the last minute. That's enough to make your teeth chatter like reindeer hooves on a tin roof.

What can send you to the malls in a blind panic? The list is long.

◆ After a prolonged bout of bah humbug, you are suddenly awash in Christmas spirit. Congratulations!

Unfortunately, it is now December 21.

◆ You get a huge, gaily wrapped package from Great Aunt Martha. And you thought she was dead.

◆ Someone does something wonderful for you when you least expect it. Your boss surprises you with a Christmas bonus. Your neighbor cuts down the dead pine in your front yard for free, actually missing your house.

◆ You were ready for Christmas three months

ago. You made a list in July, shopped in August, and wrapped in September. Alas, you just got an attack of the annual Christmas terrors: *I didn't get enough!*

◆ You are, by preference and principle, as committed to procrastination as is a grizzly bear to her new-born cub. Now the awful truth has hit home: yet again, they are not going to postpone Christmas until you're ready.

Now, about the malls: by this time there's nothing on the shelves but the expensive and the wildly inappropriate. You need help. You need either an army of elves or some great ideas for good-looking, make-it-yourself, quick and easy presents. Since elves are hard to come by this late in the season, you might want to peruse the following pages, where you'll find hand-crafted gifts to please everyone on your late list.

Last-Minute ❧
Christmas Gifts

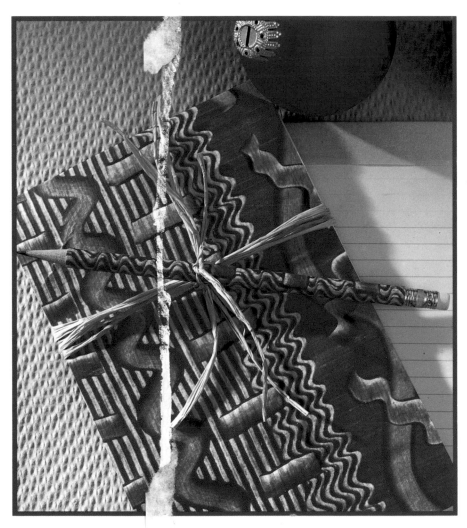

*Crafting
Quick & Classy
Presents for
Everyone
on Your List*

❧

Carol Taylor

Sterling Publishing Co., Inc.   New York
A STERLING/LARK BOOK

Art Director, Illustrations, and Production: Chris Colando
Photography: Evan Bracken

10 9 8 7 6 5 4 3 2 1

A Sterling/Lark Book

Published by Sterling Publishing Company, Inc.
387 Park Avenue South, New York, NY 10016

Created and produced by Altamont Press, Inc.
67 Broadway, Asheville, NC 28801

© 1995, Altamont Press

The projects in this book are the original creations of the contributing designers, who retain the copyrights to their designs. The projects may be reproduced by individuals for personal pleasure; reproduction on a larger scale with the intent of personal profit is prohibited.

Distributed in Canada by Sterling Publishing
c/o Canadian Manda Group, One Atlantic Avenue, Suite 105
Toronto, Ontario, Canada M6K 3E7
Distributed in Australia y Capricorn Link (Australia) Pty. Ltd.
P.O. Box 704, Windsor, NSW 2756, Australia

Every effort has been made to ensure that all the information in this book is accurate. However, due to differing conditions, tools, and individual skills, the publisher cannot be responsible for any injuries, losses, or other damages that may result from the use of the information in this book.

Sterling ISBN 1-4027-0104-7

LEVEL OF DIFFICULTY

Most of the projects in this book require no prior knowledge whatever. You can make the spiral bracelet even if you've never been inside a bead store in your life. You can complete any of the painted gifts without the slightest experience.

Two chapters require the most elementary skills imaginable. The sewing projects assume you can machine-stitch a straight seam or that you have actually held a needle in your hand at some time in your life. The two woodworking projects assume that you have (or can borrow) a saw of some kind and a power drill with a couple of bits.

ESTIMATED TIME

The directions for each project include an estimate of how long you'll need to complete it. While that will vary from person to person, the estimate is generous enough to cover most of us.

SHOPPING TIPS

Virtually all of the materials used in the projects are widely available. Because time is at a premium, we've included a list of likely sources for any materials that might be unfamiliar to you.

ENCOURAGING WORDS

A gift you've made yourself really does carry an extra measure of warmth and good will—the essence of the season. You don't have to be the super-organized, plan-way-ahead type to participate in all this good feeling, nor do you need endless hours.

So it's late. So what? Take it from a confirmed, *now*-I've-got-the-spirit procrastinator with long-lived aunts and neighbors who wield a mean chain saw: you can still join in and celebrate the season.

NATURAL MATERIALS

While traditional Christmas greenery is wonderful—who could tire of evergreens and poinsettias?—it's nice to strike a different note with dried flowers and herbs. When Christmas cheer is past, we'll be smack in the middle of a cold, gray January, to be followed by the ever-popular February. Spring is a *long* way away. Dried flowers will be very welcome, very shortly.

Most craft stores carry a splendid assortment of natural materials, and if you're not looking for boughs of holly, you can probably find what you need even at the last minute. Florists keep dried materials on hand and can usually be persuaded to part with some.

Rose and Cedar Wreath

*a*n elegant version of traditional red and green, this wreath will be welcome long after the holiday season is past.

EST. TIME: 1½ HOURS

MATERIALS

    5-inch (12.5 cm) grapevine wreath base

    Fresh or preserved cedar sprigs

    Dried red roses

    2 yards (1.8 m) wired velvet ribbon

TOOLS

    Glue gun

    Floral wire

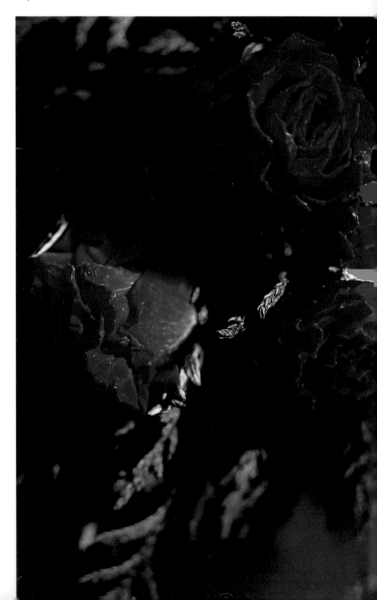

1. Starting on the inside of the wreath and working to the outside edge, hot-glue cedar sprigs to the wreath base, pointing the tips in the same direction to form a spiral. Make sure the base is completely covered and that no glue is visible.

2. Hot-glue the roses to the base in groups of three.

3. Shape the ribbon into a bow with streamers and wire it around the center to hold it together.

4. To make a hanger, fold a 16-inch (40.5 cm) piece of ribbon in half and twist the ends together. Wire one end of the loop to the back of the wreath. Wire the bow to the other end of the hanger.

DESIGN: Diane Weaver

Winter Garden

*L*iving greenery is a joy in midwinter. A thriving bed of succulents—fleshy, moisture-conserving plants—will delight your winter-bound friends. Look for succulents in nurseries and home improvement stores with good garden sections.

EST. TIME: ½ HOUR

MATERIALS

  Planter

  Potting soil

  Assorted succulents

1. Fill the planter with potting soil.

2. Carefully remove the plants from their individual pots and arrange them in the planter.

3. Water sparingly.

Pinecone Fire Starters

*N*othing warms the heart (and the feet) like a roaring fire, and these pinecones will set even the stubbornest logs ablaze. A perfect gift for friends with fireplaces.

EST. TIME: 2 HOURS (counting cooling times)

MATERIALS

Newspaper

Waxed paper

2 pounds (.9 kg) paraffin

3 red crayons or red candle tint (or other colors)

1 teaspoon cinnamon oil (optional)

Pinecones

Basket

Ribbon

Evergreens

TOOLS

Double boiler or coffee can

Tongs

1. Cover your work area completely with newspaper, then with a layer of waxed paper.

2. Break the paraffin into chunks and melt it over hot water in a double boiler. Alternatively, put the wax in a clean coffee can and set it in a pan of hot water.

CAUTION: Paraffin is extremely flammable. Never heat it over an open flame or directly over any heat source. It may catch fire if you do. Never leave heating paraffin unattended.

3. Add crayons or candle tint (peel the paper label off the crayon first) until you're pleased with the color. Add the cinnamon oil.

4. Remove the paraffin from the heat. Using tongs, dip a pinecone into the paraffin for a few seconds. Gently lift it out without shaking off any excess wax. Allow the cone to cool for a few seconds, then set it on the waxed paper. Repeat with remaining cones.

5. After the cones are completely cool, dip them again. For second and subsequent dippings, keep the paraffin as cool as possible while keeping it liquid. Too-hot wax will melt off the residue from previous dippings.

6. Dip the cones as often as you want, until the wax is as thick as you want.

7. Arrange the cones in a basket along with a few sprigs of evergreens. Add a ribbon to the handle.

8. At the risk of sounding like an edgy aunt, caution the recipient not to store the coated cones too close to the fireplace. They really are fire starters—inside or outside the fireplace.

DESIGN: Bill Parker

SHOPPING TIPS

Paraffin: hardware stores and wherever home can-
ning supplies are sold. Candle tints: craft stores
that carry candle-making supplies. Cinnamon oil:
craft stores.

Prism Ornaments

Christmas tree ornaments are ever-popular Christmas gifts. These are based on prisms for chandeliers (available at lighting and home improvement stores). After the tree is gone, they can hang in a sunny window, casting rainbows around the room.

EST. TIME: ½ HOUR

MATERIALS

Monofilament (fishing line)

Prism

10-inch (25 cm) length of chiffon-type ribbon

Strands of wispy fern

Dried flowers

TOOLS

Scissors

Glue gun

1. Cut a piece of monofilament 12 inches (30 cm) long. Thread it through the metal ring on top of the prism and tie the line in a double knot right against the ring, leaving two long ends.

2. Make a bow with the ribbon and tie it onto the prism with the long pieces of monofilament. Tie the ends of the monofilament together, to make a loop for hanging.

3. Hot-glue the fern and flowers to the center of the bow.

DESIGN: Alyce Nadeau

Floral Magnets

*P*erfect for refrigerator or metal filing cabinet, these easy-to-make magnets will hold notes and photos with style. ("Buy milk... reserve Caribbean cruise... accept Pulitzer...")

EST. TIME: 1 HOUR

MATERIALS

Metal lids from cans of frozen juice

Dried greenery, flowers, and moss

Heavy-duty craft magnets

TOOLS

Glue gun

Clippers

1. Hot-glue small pieces of greenery to the can lid, covering it completely. For a full, three-dimensional effect, position some of the sprigs so that they project upward out of the base.

DESIGN: Josena McCaig

2. Starting with the larger varieties, hot-glue the flowers to the greenery. Fill in as needed with moss, nestling it between the flowers.

3. Place the magnet on the back of the metal lid. It will stay without any further effort on your part.

Miniature Wreath Pin

brighten someone's winter day with this promise of spring. The pin in the photo has plumosa fern, red rosebuds, white German statice, purple salvia, and golden yarrow, but any small, colorful dried flowers would do.

EST. TIME: ½ HOUR

MATERIALS

Vine wreath base 2 or 3 inches (5 or 7.5 cm) in diameter

Wispy strands of dried fern

Small, colorful, dried flowers

Metal pin back (available at craft and bead stores)

TOOLS

Glue gun

1. Hot-glue the ferns around the wreath, with the foliage pointing in the same direction to create a spiral pattern.

2. Starting with the larger blooms, hot-glue the flowers to the wreath.

3. Hot-glue the pin back to the back of the wreath.

DESIGN: Alyce Nadeau

15

Decorated Soap

*f*or an instant present, dress up a bar of good-quality soap with a pretty ribbon and a few dried flowers.

EST. TIME: ½ HOUR

MATERIALS

  Bar of soap

  Ribbon

  Dried flowers and
    greenery

TOOLS

  Glue gun

1. Wrap the ribbon around the soap, as you would wrap a package. Finish with a bow.

2. Hot-glue the flowers and greenery around the bow.

DESIGN: Josena McCaig

Herbal Bath Oil

*d*ry wintertime skin welcomes a scented, slippery bath. Make your own distinctive brew for a fraction of the cost of ho-hum, seen-them-everywhere varieties.

EST. TIME: ½ HOUR

MATERIALS

¾ cup (177 ml) jojoba oil

2 teaspoons essential oil: basil, bay, eucalyptus, lavender, lemon, lemongrass, rose, rose geranium, mint, pine, rosemary, sandalwood, jasmine, or patchouli (or a combination)

Decorative bottles with tight-fitting tops

Wired ribbon

Flower petals or herb sprigs to match the essential oil (optional)

SHOPPING TIPS

Jojoba oil: health food store. Essential oils: health food store, craft store, or bath shop.

NOTE: If you can't find jojoba oil, you can substitute mineral oil. Add a little Vitamin E as a preservative.

DESIGN: Kim Tibbals

1. Combine the oils and pour them into bottles. Add flower petals or sprigs of herbs if desired. Cover tightly.

2. Trim bottle with ribbon.

3. Store in a dark place.

4. Add instructions to the bottle: "Shake before using. Add 2 teaspoons (10 ml) to the bathtub."

Lavender-Scented Bath Salts

*t*he Romans scented their soaps and bath salts with lavender, and we've been soaking with this fragrant herb ever since.

EST. TIME: ½ HOUR

MATERIALS

    1 cup (237 ml) baking soda

    1 quart (1 l) epsom salts

    1 cup (237 ml) dried lavender flowers

    ½ ounce (15 ml) oil of lavender

    Decorative bottle

SHOPPING TIPS

    Lavender blossoms and oil of lavender: health food stores and specialty bath shops.

1. Place a spoonful or two of the soda in a small bowl. Add the oil of lavender. Stir and mash until blended. (A mortar and pestle work especially well.)

2. Place the mixture in a large bowl and add remaining ingredients, mixing thoroughly. Spoon the mixture into a decorative bottle and trim with raffia and lavender blooms, if desired.

3. Accompany the salts with these directions: "Sprinkle about ½ cup (118 ml) under hot, running water."

DESIGN: Alyce   Nadeau
and   Josena   McCaig

Garlic Swag

Widely available at specialty food stores and farmers' markets, garlic braids can be quickly enhanced with a few herbs and flowers. They make welcome gifts for committed cooks, who can break off bulbs as needed.

EST. TIME: ½ HOUR

MATERIALS

Length of braided garlic

Raffia or heavy string

Webbed ribbon

Bay leaves

Sprigs of dried flowers, such as safflower and lavender

Bright berries, such as pepperberries

TOOLS

Heavy scissors

Glue gun

1. If necessary, trim the stems ends of the garlic so that they're even.

2. Tie raffia or string around the "neck" of the braid and use the ends to form a loop in back for hanging.

3. Make a bow from the webbed ribbon and tie it around the swag.

4. Hot-glue the bay leaves, flowers, and berries to the swag, tucking the stems under the bow.

Moss-Covered Box

*n*o one will forget which present is yours, or confuse it with someone else's. This unique box will thrill gardeners and nature lovers who have temporarily come in from the cold. Small pieces of moss can be combined to make the total amount needed.

DESIGN: Josena McCaig

EST. TIME: 1½ HOURS

MATERIALS

    10 feet (3 m) of green moss as wide as the box

    Paper mache box

    Floral wire

    4 yards (3.7 m) wired ribbon

    Dried ferns or other greenery

    Dried flowers, such as hydrangea and lavender

TOOLS

    Glue gun

    Scissors

1. To attach the moss to the box, cover the back of the moss with generous amounts of hot glue and press the moss onto the box, covering all sides and the lid, both inside and out. Cover about 3 or 4 inches (7.5 to 10 cm) of moss at a time and press it to the box; then proceed to the next 3 or 4 inches.

2. Hot-glue one end of the ribbon to an inside wall of the box, positioning it in the center of the wall. Bring the ribbon up the inner wall, down the outside, around the bottom, up the other side, and down inside the box, all the way to the bottom.

Hot-glue the other end of the ribbon in place. Repeat with the other two sides of the box, to get the perpendicular ribbons of a typical Christmas present. Wrap ribbon around the box's lid in both directions, tying it on top.

3. Make a bow with tails and wire it together around the center; then wire it to the crossed ribbons on top of the box.

4. Decorate the top with the dried flowers and greenery, hot-gluing the stems under and around the bow. Hot-glue sprigs of flowers and greenery around the box, positioning them near the bottom.

SIMPLE SEWING

No one should expect too much of you during the Christmas season. Especially when you're running behind. That's why the projects in this chapter presume only that you can sew a (more or less) straight seam with a sewing machine, or that at some time in your life you were on speaking terms with a needle and thread. If you're unsure of yourself, remember that sales people in fabric stores are matched only by reference librarians in their cheerful determination to help.

Beaded Gloves

a scattering of beads can turn an ordinary pair of gloves into a memorable gift. Use a needle with a small eye (so it will go through the beads) and a ball (rounded) point, so it will pass between the strands of yarn rather than piercing them.

EST. TIME: 1½ HOURS

MATERIALS

    Purchased knitted gloves

    High-quality sewing thread

    Assorted beads, sequins, and other decorations

TOOLS

    Pencil and paper

    Short, small-eyed, ballpoint sewing needle

1. With paper and pencil, sketch out a design for the beads. Keep it simple; you'll need to reverse it to a mirror image on the other glove.

2. If desired, add a few tailor's tacks (obvious knots of thread) on the glove to use as guides in attaching the beads.

3. Using a doubled, knotted thread, sew the beads to the gloves, starting from the inside out.

4. End and knot the thread and start with a new one as many times as seem appropriate. (Large stitches on the inside of the glove will be fine, but gigantic ones will be a nuisance for the wearer.)

DESIGN: Judith Robertson

SEWING TIPS

◆ Keep the thread between the beads fairly loose, so that the gloves remain flexible.

◆ If a bead is particularly large-holed or heavy, you may need to sew through it twice to anchor it firmly to the glove.

Place Mats With Decorative Stitching

*P*re-quilted fabric is available in just about any fabric store. Stitch along the convenient lines in a contrasting color to make a set of distinctive place mats.

EST. TIME: 20 TO 45 MINUTES per mat (depending on amount of stitching)

MATERIALS

For four place mats:

⅔ yard (61 cm) of 45-inch (114.5 cm) pre-quilted fabric in a solid color

⅔ yard of 45-inch plain fabric (if your pre-quilted fabric is not finished on the back)

3 yards (2.8 m) of wide, double-fold bias tape

Regular sewing thread to match fabric

Heavy-weight decorative rayon thread

TOOLS

Pencil

Sewing machine

Bobbin designed to accommodate heavy thread

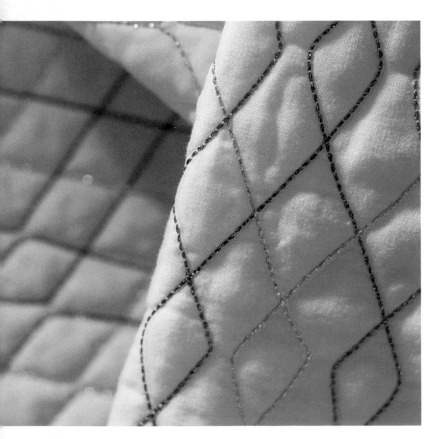

1. Cut four pieces of quilted fabric 13 inches by 18 inches (33 x 45.5 cm). If the quilted fabric is not reversible, also cut four pieces of plain fabric the same size.

2. Bias binding will be easier to attach if the corners of the place mats are somewhat rounded. Draw rounded edges on the mats and cut along these lines, trying mightily to make the mats symmetrical. (The safest approach is to draw a paper template and lay it over each mat before you cut.)

3. You'll be stitching with the decorative thread in the bobbin and with the material right side down.

Loosen the bobbin tension on your sewing machine to compensate for the heavy decorative thread. Wind a bobbin with each color you plan to use.

4. Beginning at one edge of the place mat, stitch along the quilted lines all the way to the other edge. Cover as many lines as you like, then switch to another color.

5. Readjust the bobbin back to its normal tension and insert a bobbin with regular sewing thread. Pair up each quilted mat with a plain piece, wrong sides together. Baste around them ¼ inch (6 mm) from the edge.

6. Trim all thread ends. Fold the bias binding over the edge of the place mat, with the narrower half on the right side of the mat. Encircle each mat with bias binding and topstitch in place close to the unfolded edge. As you near your starting place, cut the tape, leaving a 1-inch (2.5 cm) overlap. Fold this end under and continue stitching.

7. If desired, stitch a decorative border on the bias tape edging

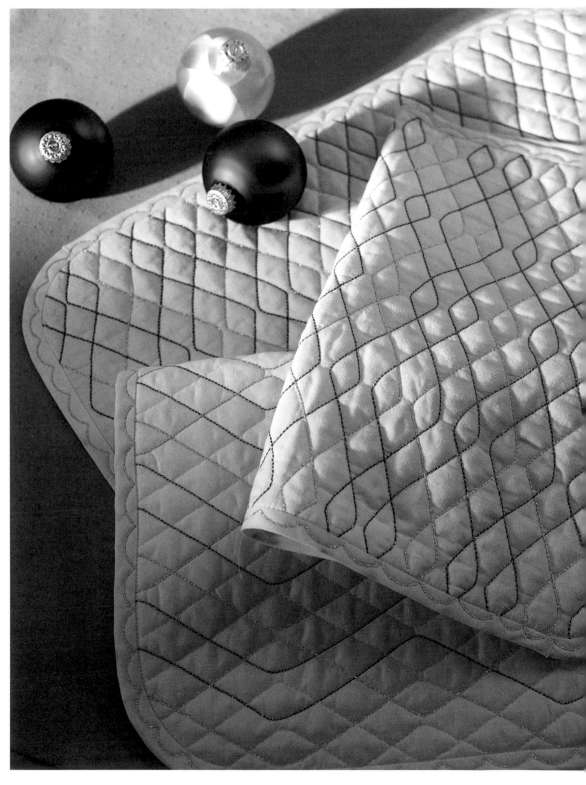

Colorful Leash and Collar

Sturdy nylon strapping—the material used for straps and fasteners on backpacks—is the body of this strong leash and adjustable collar. Fun-loving fabric is the soul.

EST. TIME: 1½ HOURS

MATERIALS

2 24-inch (61 cm) strips of dog-friendly fabric 1¼ inches (3 cm) wide

2 7-foot (2.1 m) strips of fabric 1¼ inches wide

3 yards (2.8 m) of nylon strapping 1 inch (2.5) wide

Double-sided fusible webbing

1-inch plastic snap buckle and 1-inch slider

Stainless steel swivel hook that will accept 1-inch strapping

Stainless steel D ring that will accept 1-inch strapping

White craft glue

TOOLS

Iron

Sewing machine

General sewing tools

1. Press under the long sides of all four fabric strips about ¼ inch (6 mm), to make strips ¾ inch (2 cm) wide.

2. Cut a 7-foot piece of strapping, for the leash. Cut a 24-inch piece of strapping, for the collar.

3. Use the iron and the fusible webbing to fuse a fabric strip onto each side of both pieces of strapping. (Follow the package instructions.)

4. Stitch along each edge of both strips, being careful to catch the fabric on both sides of the strapping.

5. To make the leash's hand grip, fold over about 9 inches (23 cm) of one end and stitch across both pieces 1 inch from the raw end. Stitch again 2 inches (5 cm) from the end. Trim raw end to ½ inch (1.5 cm). Seal edges with glue.

6. Thread the other end of the leash through the swivel hook and fold the end back on itself. Stitch together 1 inch from the swivel hook and again 2 inches from the hook. Trim raw end to ½ inch and seal the edges with glue.

DESIGN: Kim Tibbals

7. Slip one end of the collar through the loop of one of the buckle halves. Fold the collar back on itself about 3 inches (7.5 cm) and stitch across both pieces 1 inch from the buckle. Slip the D-ring between the pieces and stitch again on the other side of the ring. (The leash will attach to the D ring.) Trim to ¼ inch and glue raw ends together.

8. Slip the other end of the collar through the slider, then through the other buckle half, then back through the slider. Adjust the collar to what looks to be a reasonable size, trim the raw edges, and seal with glue.

SHOPPING TIPS

Nylon strapping, plastic buckle and slider: camping or outdoor store. Swivel hook and D ring: hardware store.

Ribbon Vest

*t*he day after Christmas, everyone you know will realize that they have nothing to wear on New Year's Eve. Forestall that anxiety with this festive vest—perfect party garb for man or woman.

EST. TIME: 1½ HOURS (stripes only);
   3½ HOURS (stripes plus weaving)

MATERIALS

   15 yards (13.5 m) of decorative ribbon 1½ inches (4 cm) wide

   Purchased vest

   Invisible nylon thread

   Fold-over braid trim

   Double-sided fusible webbing

TOOLS

   Sewing machine

   Standard sewing tools

1. Remove buttons from purchased vest.

2. **For long strips of ribbon** (see the back and the left front): Lay the ribbons on the vest in whatever pattern you like, and pin them into place. Cut each piece of ribbon even with the edge of the vest.

3. Topstitch the ribbons along each long edge. If the ribbons cross over each other, don't sew across the ribbon that's on top. When you come to a cross piece, lift the presser foot, advance the fabric until you're across the barrier, and start sewing again. Come back later and cut off the long piece of thread that crosses the ribbon. To prevent raveling, adjust the machine to sew very tiny stitches before and after each jump.

   For woven ribbons (see right front): If the ribbons will tolerate being ironed on the wool setting (test a piece first), the easiest approach is to first weave the ribbons, then fuse them to the vest with double-sided fusible webbing.

4. To begin, measure the length of the vest and cut ribbons about 2 inches (5 cm) longer than that. Position these vertical ribbons side by side, edges touching, until they're an inch or two wider

Ribbon Vest

If your ribbons can't stand the heat, weave them directly on the vest, pinning the vertical ribbons to the vest and then weaving the horizonal ones. Trim all ribbon ends even with the edges of the vest, then topstitch around the edge of the vest, securing the ribbons in place.

6. Fold the braid over the edges of the vest, with the narrow side to the front. Topstitch close to the edge of the vest, making sure to catch both sides of the braid and the fabric in between. Sew the buttons onto the vest.

NOTE: If you plan to make the vest, apply the ribbons to the front and back pieces before joining them.

ALSO NOTE: If you don't want to finish the edges of the vest with fold-over braid, cut the ribbon pieces ½ inch (1.5 cm) longer than the edge of the vest. Fold under each ribbon end as you sew it down.

than you'll need. Pin the ends to your work surface. (A padded ironing board works well.) Starting at the top, weave ribbons horizontally over and under the vertical ones. Make sure the horizontal ribbons alternate which vertical ribbons they go over and which they go under.

5. Follow the package instructions to iron the webbing onto the ribbons, then the ribbons onto the vest. Trim the ribbons even with all edges of the vest.

Reversible Holiday Apron

*e*arn extra (ahem) brownie points with this apron. Since it's reversible, it can be worn year-round. While lining an apron may seem like overkill, it's actually faster than hemming.

EST. TIME: 2 HOURS (not counting pre-laundering)

MATERIALS

    1 yard (.9 m) cotton print 45 inches (114 cm) wide

    1 yard solid color cotton 45 inches wide

    Sewing thread to match fabric

    3½ yards (3.2 m) double-fold bias tape

    Metallic thread for decorative stitching (optional)

TOOLS

    Sewing machine

    Scissors

    Measuring tape

1. Wash, dry, and press both fabrics to preshrink them.

2. Enlarge the pattern on a photocopier or use the drawing to make an enlargement on gridded pattern-drafting material. Or draw a freehand pattern. (This isn't brain surgery.)

3. Fold the fabrics lengthwise and cut one apron piece from each.

4. Cut one piece of bias tape 11 inches (28 cm) long, to bind the top of the bib, and one approximately 3 yards (2.7 m) long, for the continuous piece that forms the ties, neck strap, and binding for the sides.

5. With right sides together, sew the main apron pieces together down the straight sides and across the bottom, using a ½-

DESIGN: Carol Parks

Reversible Holiday Apron

inch (1.5 cm) seam allowance. Trim the corners, turn the apron right sides out, and press. Topstitch around the finished edges. Stitch the upper raw edges together, sewing ¼ inch (6 mm) from the edge.

6. Press both pieces of bias tape so that the center fold is slightly toward one edge.

7. Fold the short piece of tape over the top of the apron's bib, with the shorter side of the tape on the right side of the apron. Sew the tape to the apron, stitching on the right side, close to the edge of the tape.

8. Find the center of the long tape; this will be the center of the neck strap. Measure 9½ inches (24 cm) from the center in each direction; pin these points to the upper corners of the apron. (Adjust the neck strap, if necessary, for a very tall or very short person.) Fold the tape

over the curved edges of the apron, with the longer side of the tape to the front, as before. With your fingers, re-press the neck strap and the apron strings so the edges of the tape are even; pin in place, if necessary. Beginning at the end of an apron string, stitch close to the edges of the tape, continuing the stitching to attach the tape to the curved sides of apron.

9. Replace the upper thread in your sewing machine with the metallic thread for decorative stitching, keeping regular thread in the bobbin. (If the metallic thread tends to shear at the needle eye, a needle designed specifically for metallic threads should solve the problem.) Choose one of the machine's decorative stitches, or use a simple zigzag stitch along the ties and binding. A honeycomb stitch was used on the apron in the photo.

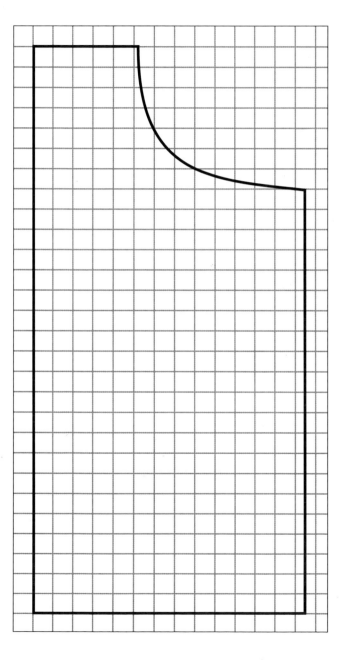

1 square = 1" (2.5 cm)

Place Mats With Bold Stripes

*F*or a graphic gift, stitch strips of bias binding onto purchased place mats. If you'd prefer to make your own mats, it's a simple matter.

Est. time: 1½ hours

Materials

Purchased place mats

1-inch-wide (2.5 cm) bias binding in contrasting colors

¾-inch (2 cm) white twill tape

Thread to match bias binding

Thread to match place mat

Fabric glue or fusible web tape

Tools

Tape measure or ruler

Sewing machine

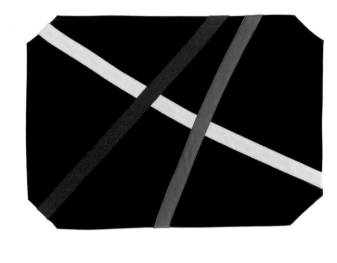

1. Decide where you want to position the various colors on the mats.

2. Cut pieces of bias binding long enough to cross the mat at the points you planned, plus 3 inches (7.5 cm) on each end. Cut pieces of twill tape the same lengths. Insert the pieces of twill tape inside the pieces of bias binding, sandwiching the tape inside the folds. (The twill tape "lining" will prevent the color of the fabric from showing through on the finished mats.)

3. Fold under ¼ inch (6 mm) of each raw end and stitch in place. Lay a bias strip in position on the mat. Fold about 1½ inches (4 cm) of one end under the edge of the mat. Stitch down the long edge of the bias strip, stitching right at the edge. As you near the other end, fold 1½ inches under the mat, then continue stitching, catching both front and back bias strips to the mat. Stitch back along the other side of the strip. Repeat with remaining bias strips.

4. On the back of the mats, seal the open ends of the bias strips with a dot of fabric glue or a small piece of fusible webbing.

DESIGN: Mary S. Parker

To Make the Mats

Est. time: 1½ hours

Materials

1 yard (91.5 cm) of fabric 60 inches (154 cm) wide

¾ yard (68.5 cm) of fusible fleece 45 inches (114.5 cm) wide

Matching thread

Fusible webbing

Tools

Measuring tape

Sewing machine

Iron

1. Cut four pieces of fabric 19½ by 14½ inches (50 x 37 cm).

2. Cut four pieces of fusible fleece 18 by 13 inches (45.5 x 33 cm).

3. To make the angled corners, mark 2 inches (5 cm) from the corner on each long side of each mat; mark 1½ inches (4 cm) from the corner on each short side. Draw lines between the marks, then cut along the line.

4. Place the glue side of the fusible fleece on the wrong side of the fabric piece. Iron to fuse, according to package instructions. Turn under the extra fabric around the fleece and iron to crease. Topstitch around the place mat ¼ inch (6 mm) from the edge.

5. Using a mat as a pattern, cut out four more pieces of fabric. Seal them to the back of the mats with fusible webbing.

Yarn-Trimmed Hat and Mittens

*a*dd a few bright stitches, and a plain, purchased hat and mittens become a festive matched set. Even if you're a novice needleworker, you can master these three simple stitches.

EST. TIME: 3 HOURS

MATERIALS

Knit hat and mittens

Crewel or needlepoint yarn in various colors

TOOLS

Pencil and paper

Crewel or needlepoint needle

Scissors

1. Briefly sketch out your design on paper, deciding which stitches go in which rows.

2. Working with one color at a time, thread the needle and knot the yarn. Start by bringing the needle from the inside of the garment to the outside. From then on, take the yarn under the knitted material, but don't go all the way through the inside lining. From row to row, alter the size of the stitches for greater variety.

VERTICAL STITCHES

Bring needle up at 1. Insert at 2. (See the green and orange stitches on the mittens.)

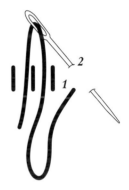

FLY STITCH

Bring needle up at 1. Insert at 2, directly across, then angle needle out at 3. Carry the yarn under the needle point and pull through. Complete stitch by inserting at 4 over the loop.

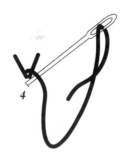

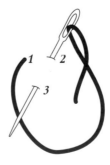

DESIGN: Ellen Zahorec

BLANKET STITCH

Bring needle out at 1.
Insert at 2, above and
slightly to the right,
then exit at 3, directly
below. Before pulling
needle all the way
through, carry yarn
under point of needle.
Proceed to next stitch.
Point 3 of previous
stitch is now point 1.

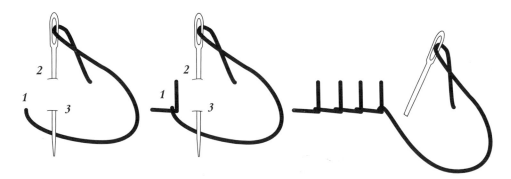

Battenberg Sachets

*e*ach of these tailored sachets began as an inexpensive place mat, pillow case, or table runner trimmed with Battenberg lace. Filled with purchased potpourri, they make fine little gifts.

EST. TIME: 1 HOUR for three sachets

MATERIALS

For each sachet:

7½-inch (19.5 cm) square of Battenberg-trimmed fabric

¼ yard (23 cm) white organza or chiffon

12 inches (30.5 cm) satin ribbon ⅛ inch (3 mm) wide

8-inch (20.5 cm) length of crochet edging

Potpourri

TOOLS

Sewing machine

Standard sewing tools

Iron

SHOPPING TIP

Crochet edging: fabric stores.

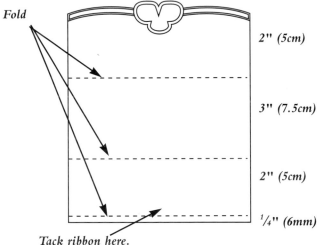

Fold

2" (5cm)

3" (7.5cm)

2" (5cm)

¼" (6mm)

Tack ribbon here.

Figure 1

1. Cut the square of Battenberg, centering the openwork trim on one edge.

2. Right side out, fold under the end opposite the trim ¼ inch (6 mm). Press. Fold another ¼ inch. Press and stitch.

3. Fold the sides under ¼ inch. Press.

4. Right side out, fold the bottom edge up 2 inches (5 cm) and press the fold. Fold the top down 2 inches and press.

5. Insert the crochet edging between the folded layers at the ends of the sachet, with the unfinished edge of the crochet strip to the inside. Sew each end of the sachet closed, stitching close to the edge, through both layers of fabric and the crochet edging.

DESIGN: Kim Tibbals

6. To make a lining that will confine the pot-pourri, cut a piece of organza or chiffon 6½ by 7 inches (16.5 x 18 cm). Fold in half on the shorter side. Stitch around the raw edges

¼ inch from the edge, leaving a 2-inch open-ing on the long side. Fill with potpourri and stitch opening closed. Insert into sachet.

7. Tack the center of the ribbon to the center of the hemmed edge of the sachet. See Figure 1. Bring the ends of the ribbon through the holes in the lace and tie in a bow.

41

Battenberg Vase

*n*apkins with Battenberg lace on one corner are fairly common. Turn one into an uncommon container for dried flowers. A loop of grosgrain ribbon can serve as a hanger or can hang below the vase to frame it.

EST. TIME: 1 HOUR

MATERIALS

    Napkin with Battenberg trim

    8 feet (2.5 m) of white grosgrain ribbon about ⅜ inch (9 mm) wide

    Fabric finish spray

    Dried flowers

TOOLS

    Iron

    Ruler or tape measure

    Pencil

    Sewing machine

1. Carefully press the napkin, using fabric finish to help remove all creases and to give it body.

2. Fold the napkin into a triangle, right side out, by bringing the lace corner to the opposite one. See Figure 1.

3. Measure to the center of the fold line and mark it with a pin. Measure out 2 inches (5 cm) on each side of the center and mark each point with a light pencil mark.

4. Measure ½ inch (1.5 cm) on each side of the Battenberg trim. Using

the pencil and ruler, draw lines to connect these marks. Cut through both layers of fabric along these lines. See Figure 2.

5. Wrong sides together, stitch the sides together ¼ inch (6 mm) from the edge. Trim the corners and turn wrong side out. Press. Stitch along the

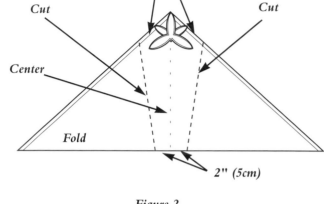

Figure 2

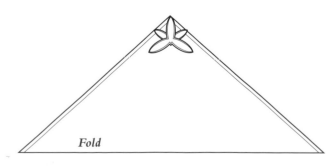

Figure 1

outside edges slightly more than ¼ inch from the edge, to seal the raw edges within the seam. Turn right side out and press, using fabric finish again. Fold down the lace corner and press.

6. Cut a 4-foot (1.2 m) length of ribbon. Find the center and tack it to the vase at the four places shown in Figure 3, leaving 2 inches of ribbon on each end to knot and notch.

7. Cut two 2-foot (61 cm) pieces of ribbon. Tie each into a simple bow and tack one on each side of the vase.

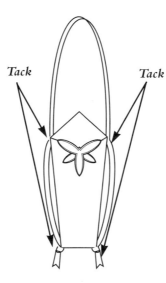

Figure 3

Sashiko Stockings

Sashiko is a time-honored Japanese embroidery technique. Traditionally, it was worked by hand—with a simple running stitch—on indigo-dyed fabrics. Modern versions use the sewing machine and any color at all.

EST. TIME: 2 TO 3 HOURS for two stockings

MATERIALS

For each stocking:

½ yard (45.5 cm) of fabric 45 inches (114.5 cm) wide

½ yard of white fusible interfacing

Tracing paper

White top-stitching thread

Thread to match fabric

Fusible web tape

TOOLS

Pencil and paper

Sewing machine and sewing supplies

Tracing paper

Dark iron-on transfer pen

Iron

1. With pencil and paper, draw an outline of the stocking, making it as large and generous as your mantle (and your wallet) will support. Allow extra for ¼-inch (6 mm) seams and a generous hem at top. Lay the paper pattern on the fabric and cut out a front and a back. Use the same pattern to cut out one piece of interfacing.

2. Make a full-size paper template of the sashiko design—that is, one large enough to cover the entire front of the stocking. To do that, trace the design block over and over onto a piece of tracing paper, joining the lines at the sides and at top and bottom to create a continuous grid.

3. Fold the top of the stocking front to the inside where you plan to hem it. Lay the stocking on the template, positioning the design lines where you want them. Trace around the stocking on the template and cut it out.

4. Using the transfer pen, mark every line on the right side of the template. Let dry.

5. Unfold the hem and fuse the interfacing to the wrong side of the stocking front, following package instructions.

6. When the marks on the template have dried, lay it, inked side down, on the interfaced side of the stocking. Use the iron to transfer the markings to the interfacing, following package instructions.

7. Fill a bobbin with the top-stitching thread. (You'll be sewing with the right side of the fabric facing down.) Adjust the bobbin's tension to accept the heavy top-stitching thread. Add regular sewing thread to the top of the machine.

8. Beginning at one edge of the stocking, stitch along a marked line all the way to the other edge. (No need to backstitch at beginning or end.)

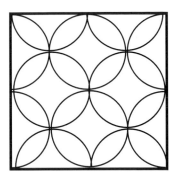

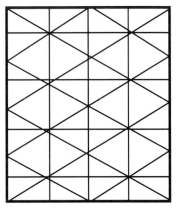

Photocopy at 240%

DESIGN: Mary S. Parker

Continue stitching long, continuous lines until you have stitched over them all. (Keep an eye on your thread; you don't want to run out in the middle of a line.)

9. When all lines are stitched, insert a bobbin with regular thread. Place the stocking front and back right sides together. Stitch around the stocking ¼ inch from the edge, leaving the top open. Clip the curves and turn the stocking right side out. Press. Zigzag or staystitch around the top to prevent raveling. Turn the hem under and press. Secure hem with fusible web tape, following the package instructions.

DESIGNING YOUR OWN

Traditional sashiko designs can be found in a number of books. It's also fun to create your own. A couple of hints:

1. Sashiko designs are based on a grid and consist of straight or curved lines. Your design should contain long, continuous lines, not a lot of short ones.

2. Sashiko is a repeat pattern—that is, the same design block repeats itself over and over. Make sure the lines on one edge meet up with the lines at the opposite edge, so the pattern can be joined side to side and top to bottom without breaking the lines.

45

Sashiko Napkin Rings and Hot Pads

White stitching on blue fabric—the traditional colors for sashiko designs.

EST. TIME: 3 HOURS

MATERIALS

For 6 napkins, 6 napkin rings, and 2 hot pads

1 yard (.9 m) solid-color fabric 60 inches (153 cm) wide

¼ yard (23 cm) fusible fleece

White top-stitching thread

Sewing thread to match fabric

Fusible web tape

Tracing paper

15 inches (38 cm) of hook-and-loop tape ¾ inch (2 cm) wide (for napkin rings)

TOOLS

Iron

Dark iron-on transfer pen

Sewing machine

Figure 2

PREP WORK

1. Load two bobbins: one with the white top-stitching thread, one with matching sewing thread.

2. Cut out six pieces of fabric 16 inches (40.5 cm) square, for the napkins; six pieces of fabric 4 by 8 inches (10 x 20.5 cm), for the napkin rings; and two pieces 12 by 16 inches (30.5 x 40.5 cm), for the hot pads. See the layout in Figure 1.

3. Cut out two pieces of fusible fleece 8 by 10 inches (20.5 x 25 cm), for the hot pads; and six pieces 2 by 7 inches (5 x 18 cm), for the napkin rings.

60-inch-wide fabric (153 cm)

16" (40.5cm)	N	N	N	HP ← 12" → (30.5cm)
16"	N	N	N	HP
	NR NR	NR NR	NR NR	

Figure 1

NAPKINS

To fringe the napkins, stitch around each 16-inch-square piece of fabric ½ inch (1.5 cm) from the edge with matching thread, pivoting at the corners. Pull a few threads to start them raveling and wash the napkins a time or two in the washing machine. Pull out any stray threads. To prevent further raveling, run a narrow zigzag stitch over the initial line of stitching.

NAPKIN RINGS

1. Zigzag along the long edges of the 4 by 8 pieces of fabric, to prevent raveling.

2. Center a 2 by 7 piece of fleece, glue side down, on the wrong side of each fabric piece; iron the pieces to fuse them; following package directions.

3. Photocopy or trace the sashiko design for the napkin rings, to make a template. See Figure 2. Using the transfer pen, mark

DESIGN: Mary S. Parker

1. Zigzag along the short edges of the hot pad pieces of fabric, to prevent raveling.

2. Fuse an 8 by 10 piece of fleece to the wrong side of each fabric piece, centering long sides and short sides.

3. Photocopy the sashiko design at 370%, or enlarge it by hand. Transfer the design to the middle of the fleece, using the template and the transfer pen. (See Step 3 for the napkin rings.)

4. Insert the bobbin with the top-stitching thread into the machine (loosening the tension on the bobbin first). With the right side of the fabric down, stitch along the marked lines, pivoting where necessary.

5. Turn the short sides of the fabric over the fleece and press; secure with fusible webbing. Fold the long sides of the fabric over the fleece and press; secure with fusible webbing.

every line on the template. Let dry. Lay the template, inked side down, on the fleece, making sure to center it. Use the iron to transfer the markings to the fleece, following package instructions. Re-ink the lines after a few napkin rings, if necessary.

4. Adjust the bobbin tension on the sewing machine to accommodate heavy thread, and insert the bobbin with the white top-stitching thread.

5. With the right side of the fabric down, stitch along the lines of the transferred design, pivoting where necessary.

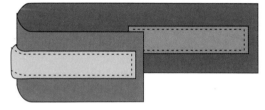

Figure 3

6. Fold the long edges of the fabric over the fleece and press. To secure the folds, place strips of fusible tape between the two layers and iron to fuse.

7. Fold each end of the fabric under ¼ inch (6 mm). Insert a bobbin with regular, matching sewing thread into the machine and stitch along the folded edge.

8. Cut six pieces of hook-and-loop tape 2½ inches (6.5 cm) long. Separate each piece into its two layers. For each napkin ring, sew the two layers on opposite ends—and opposite sides—of the napkin ring. See Figure 3. Put the hook (soft) layer on the outside of the ring and the loop (bristly) layer on the inside.

Man's Wallet

*t*his compact, soft-sided wallet has room for folding money (not necessarily included) and nine credit cards (definitely not included).

Man's Wallet

EST. TIME: 1½ HOURS

MATERIALS

Piece of upholstery fabric, or other heavy fabric, 4¾ by 9½ inches (12 x 24.5 cm)

½ yard (45.5 cm) cotton fabric

5 inches (12.5 cm) hook-and-loop fastener ¾ inch (2 cm) wide

1 yard (.9 m) grosgrain ribbon ¾ inch wide

TOOLS

Iron

Sewing machine

Standard sewing tools

1. Lay the upholstery fabric wrong side up. Fold it lengthwise into three sections: 3 inches (7.5 cm), for the front of the wallet; 3⅜ inches (8.5 cm), for the back; and 3⅛ inches (8 cm), for the inside flap. See Figure 1. Press the folds to crease them.

2. On the right side of the inside flap, place the soft portion of the hook-and-loop tape so that it runs vertically, with the left edge of the tape 1¾ inches (4.5 cm) from the edge of the fabric. See Figure 2. Stitch around the edge of the tape.

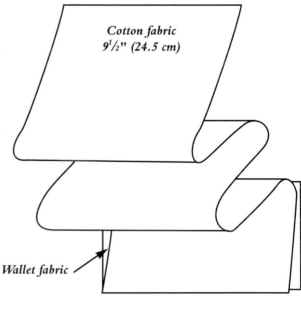

Cotton fabric 9½" (24.5 cm)

Wallet fabric

Figure 3

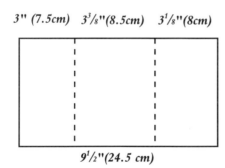

3" (7.5cm)   3⅜"(8.5cm)   3⅛"(8cm)

9½"(24.5 cm)

Figure 1

Figure 2

3. Cut a piece of cotton fabric 4¾ by 9½ inches. Wrong sides together, baste it to the upholstery fabric, stitching close to the edges.

4. Cut a piece of cotton fabric 9½ by 24 inches (12 x 61 cm). This will fold up accordion-style to create rows of pockets for credit cards. To begin, place the wallet wrong side up on the ironing board. Position the cotton fabric as shown in Figure 3, with the sides and bottom edges lined up. Fold the cotton down 1 inch below the top

3" (7.5cm)   3³⁄₈"(8.5cm)   3¹⁄₈"(8cm)

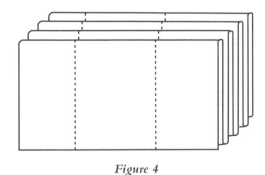

Figure 4

edge of the wallet; press to crease. Fold the cotton back up ½ inch (1.5 cm) from the bottom edge; press. Press down again ¼ inch (6 mm) below the first crease; press

up again ¼ inch from the bottom edge. Press down again ¼ inch below second top crease; press up again at bottom edge. Press down ¼ inch below third crease.

Trim off any excess fabric to make bottom edges even.

5. Remove the accordion filler from the wallet and stitch two seams as shown in Figure 4, going through all thicknesses.

6. Stitching close to the edges, machine baste the accordion filler to the inside of the wallet, being sure folds and seams align. The filler will be shorter than the wallet top to bottom, to leave room

at the top for bills.

7. Position the loop portion of the tape on the inside left fold of the wallet, folding and checking to be sure it aligns with the other strip. Stitch along the long edges.

8. Press the ribbon in half lengthwise. Fold it over the raw edges of the wallet and top-stitch it in place, beginning and ending on the inside flap.

Tapestry Tote

a flat-bottomed tote bag will be welcomed by anyone with clutter to carry: knitters, grocery shoppers, or new parents. Office workers will pack it every morning with lunch, diet drink, and the papers they took home and ignored the night before.

EST. TIME: 1 HOUR

MATERIALS

   ½ yard (45.5 cm) of tapestry or other sturdy fabric

   2 yards (1.8 m) webbing

   Thread

TOOLS

   Standard sewing tools

   Sewing machine

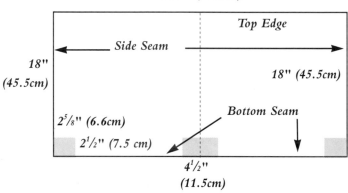

36¾" (93.5cm)

Top Edge

Side Seam

18"
(45.5cm)

18" (45.5cm)

Bottom Seam

2⅝" (6.6cm)

2½" (7.5 cm)

4½"
(11.5cm)

Figure 1

1. Cut the fabric 18 inches long by 36¾ inches wide (45.5 x 93.5 cm).

2. Cut out the three shaded rectangles shown on Figure 1. Each corner rectangle should be 2½ inches (7.5 cm) high and 2⅝ inches (6.6 cm) wide. The center rectangle is 2½ inches high and 4½ inches (11.5 cm) wide.

3. To prevent raveling, staystitch or zigzag all edges of the fabric.

4. With right sides together, fold the fabric in half width-wise. Sew up the side seam, using a standard ⅝-inch (1.5 cm) seam. Press the seam to one side and top-stitch it down, so that it lies flat.

5. Right sides together, sew the bottom seam together between the rectangles, using a ⅜-inch (1.5 cm) seam.

You'll be left with two unjoined areas on your tote.

6. With the bag still inside out, insert both index fingers into one of the openings at the bottom. Pull the front of the bag away from the back. The bottom of the bag will cooperatively fold up and meet the sides. (Trust us.) Pin the bottom to the sides, right sides together, and sew them together with a ⅜-inch seam. Repeat for the other open corner.

7. Press under a 3-inch (7.5 cm) hem all around the top of the tote.

8. Cut the webbing into two pieces, each 1 yard (.9 m) long. Measure out 4 inches (10 cm) from the center of the tote. At that point, insert one end of a webbing piece under the hem as far as it will go. Pin in place. Insert the other end of the webbing under the hem on the opposite side of the bag and pin in place. Repeat for other piece of webbing, positioning it 4 inches from the center as you did the first.

9. Check that the webbing lies flat and untwisted. Topstitch the entire hem in place, catching the pieces of webbing in the seam as you come to them.

10. Fold the webbing up over the seam so that it extends up from the bag and forms a handle on each side. Working on the wrong side of the bag, topstitch two parallel lines on the webbing, from the top of the bag down 2¾ inches (7 cm), catching both the visible layer of webbing and the hem, for extra security.

Paisley Beret

*S*tave off those cold winter winds with a wool beret appliquéd with paisley designs (or whatever shapes you choose). Even if you don't know how to embroider, the stitch is so simple that a rank beginner can do it with ease.

EST. TIME: 3 HOURS

MATERIALS

  Purchased wool beret

  Scraps of wool or wool felt

  Perle cotton or embroidery floss in contrasting colors

  Fusible webbing (optional)

TOOLS

  Pencil and paper

  Scissors

  Sharp embroidery needle

  Straight pins

1. Draw paper patterns for the large and small paisley shapes. Lay the patterns on the wool scraps and cut out as many appliqués as you think you might need.

2. Sew the small paisley shapes to the large ones, using a simple blanket stitch. (See the illustrations.)

3. Pin the paisleys to the beret, arranging them any way you like.

4. For easier stitching, cut a small square of fusible webbing for each appliqué, place it between the appliqué and the beret, and iron in place, following the package instructions.

5. Using a simple blanket stitch, sew each appliqué to the beret. Depending upon your (and the recipient's) tastes, use either small, tightly spaced stitches or larger, more graphic ones.

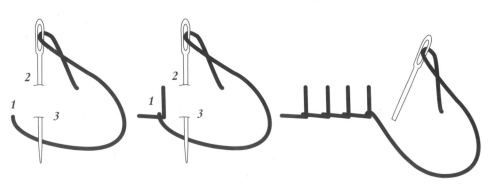

Blanket Stitch

Butterfly Appliqué Vest

ost fabric stores with classes on sewing ultrasuede (or with in-house seamstresses) have an ultrasuede scrap bin. Dig in! If one isn't handy, other fabrics can be used for the appliqués and fused to the vest with double-sided fusible web.

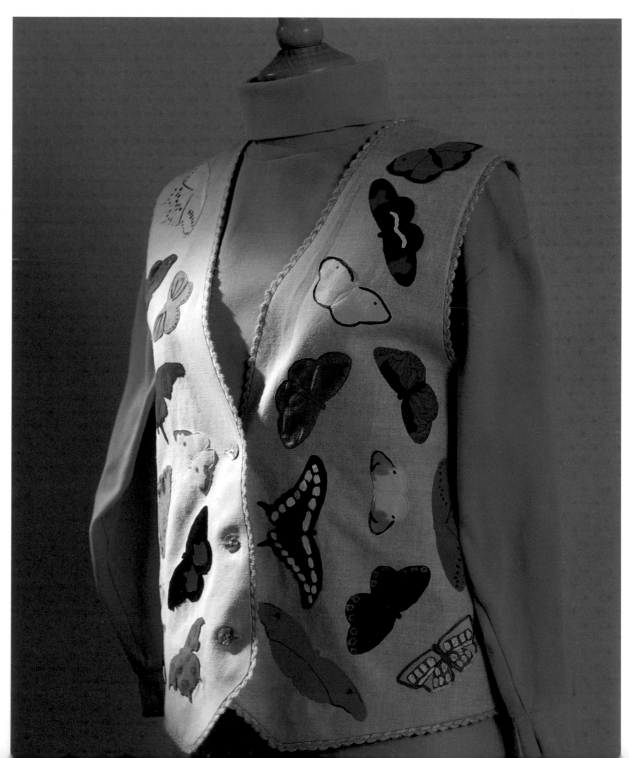

EST. TIME: 4 HOURS

MATERIALS

Paper

Scraps of ultrasuede

Fabric markers or fabric paints and a small
paint brush

Purchased vest

Fabric glue

TOOLS

Pen or pencil

Scissors

1. Draw some butterflies on paper. If you prefer to trace them from other sources, check nature books or magazines, or even children's coloring books. Cut out the butterflies, leaving extra paper on all sides.

2. Lay each paper pattern on a piece of ultrasuede and pin in place. Cut along the traced lines, cutting through both paper and fabric. (Cutting them together helps keep the ultrasuede from shifting.)

3. Decorate each butterfly with markers or paints and let dry. If you like, check a field guide to butterflies out of the local library and use it for inspiration.

4. Arrange the butterflies on the vest to your satisfaction.

5. Working one butterfly at a time, apply a thin, even coating of fabric glue to the backs of the appliqués, making sure there's no excess glue to ooze out the sides. Press each butterfly firmly in place.

NOTE: If you'd rather sew than glue, attach each appliqué with a dot of fabric glue to hold it in position, and let dry. Stitch around the appliqués with invisible nylon thread, working very close to the edges.

PAPER PRESENTS

Those of us who love books tend to love fine paper as well. The most versatile of materials, it can be painted to suit any taste, cut into bookmarks, folded into boxes or napkin rings, sewn into simple books, and treated in a hundred other ways.

Embellished Books

*b*lank books with soft corrugated covers and earthy brown pages are found at paper supply, art supply, and craft stores. Spruced up with ribbon and a decoration or two, they become unique. The brown book sports a brooch from a thrift shop (the pin back was snipped off with wire cutters). The leaves on the red book are from a craft store's grab bin.

EST. TIME: ½ HOUR

MATERIALS

Blank paper books

Heavy metallic embroidery thread

White craft glue

Grosgrain ribbon

Waxed paper

Small, lightweight decorations

TOOLS

Large-eyed needle

Scissors

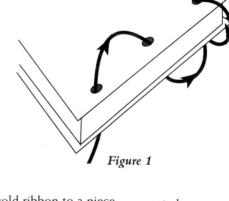

Figure 1

1. Remove the string binding from the book (shown on the book at left). Starting from an end hole and working from the back of the book, re-sew the binding with the metallic embroidery thread, using a simple running stitch. Go through each end hole three times, in order to loop the thread around the end and around the side. See Figure 1. Tie off the thread on the back of the book.

2. Cut a length of ribbon slightly shorter than the book is long and glue it lightly to the book. (For the red book shown, glue a piece of open-weave gold ribbon to a piece of red grosgrain ribbon; then glue both to the book.) Cover with a scrap of waxed paper and weight with a heavy book for about 1 hour.

3. Glue and/or sew the decoration to the ribbon. If desired, add some decorative stitches around the centerpiece, using the metallic thread.

4. Pierce the front and back covers very close to the edge of the open side of the book. Thread a doubled length of metallic thread through both holes and tie in a bow.

DESIGN: Terry Taylor

Folded Paper Napkin Rings

*e*ven people who rarely use (and don't own) napkin rings enjoy them for special occasions—Christmas dinner, for example. These rings of folded paper will delight their new owners through many a meal.

DESIGN: Terry Taylor

EST. TIME: 2 HOURS for 6 rings

MATERIALS

Medium to heavy paper (wrapping paper, origami paper, even pages from home decorating or art magazines)

TOOLS

Ruler

Pencil

Scissors

1. Cut 16 pieces of paper 4½ by 2 inches (11.5 x 5 cm).

2. Fold one of the cut pieces in half lengthwise. "Sharpen" the fold by laying the pencil flat on top of it and pushing the pencil up and down the crease. Sharpen all folds in this way. Unfold.

3. Bring each long edge to the center crease. Press. Fold along the center crease. Press. Your paper will now be ½ inch by 4½ inches (1.5 x 11.5 cm). See Figure 1.

4. Fold the piece in half end to end and crease the fold. Unfold.

5. Bring each short end to the center crease. Fold and crease the folds. See Figure 2.

Figure 1

Figure 2

6. Make a total of 16 of these paper "links."

7. To begin joining the pieces, lay one link on edge. (It's easier if the folded edges are on top.) Insert the ends of a second link into the folded sides of the first. Each "leg" of the second link should be sandwiched between the double walls of the first. See Figure 3. Fit the two corners snugly together so that you have a V shape. See Figure 4.

8. Insert a third link the same way into the second one, pointing it in

the opposite direction from the first, creating a zigzag pattern. Continue until you have used 15 links.

9. Now to link the two ends to form a ring. (This is not hard.) Unfold the last unused link—good old #16—once, to make a piece ½ inch by 2¼ inches (1.5 x 5.5cm). Add it to the previous link in the usual way, pulling it tight. Now bring the two ends of the napkin ring together and insert the long ends of link #16 into link #1. Fold the ends

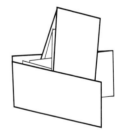

Figure 3

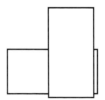

Figure 4

of #16 around the outside of #1 and insert them back into #15.

Sponged Paper Place Mats

When they're laminated by an office supply or quick-print shop, paper place mats are durable and easy to clean. The ones shown were sponge-painted in off-white, dark blue, and medium blue-green (with some dull gold accents on the mat below), but colors can match any decor. Choose paper that's tough enough to stand up to several coats of paint.

EST. TIME: 1 HOUR (not counting drying time)

MATERIALS

Heavy rag paper

White water-based primer

Latex or acrylic paint in desired colors

Paper tape (or other low-sticky tape that won't mar the paint or tear the paper)

Water-based glazing liquid (optional)

TOOLS

2-inch (5 cm) latex paint brush

Straight-edge or yardstick

Pencil

Scissors or matte knife

Natural sea sponge

Feather (optional)

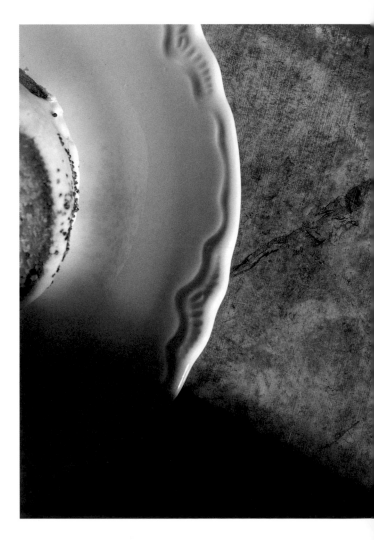

1. Brush a coat of primer on the paper and allow to dry.

2. Measure and cut the place mats. Most are about 11 by 17 inches (28 x 43 cm).

3. Apply a second coat of primer. If you want a base coat in some color other than white, apply it instead. Let dry.

4. Thin the latex paint you plan to use for sponging. (If you're using several colors, work from the darkest to the lightest.) Try a mixture of $\frac{2}{3}$ paint and $\frac{1}{3}$ water; if that's too thick, add more water. For more transparent glazing, try a mixture of $\frac{1}{3}$ paint, $\frac{1}{3}$ glazing liquid, and $\frac{1}{3}$ water.

5. Pour a little of the thinned paint onto a paper plate, a square of aluminum foil, or a jar lid. Dampen the sponge and wring out excess water. Dip the sponge in the paint and press it on the place mat. Continue until you've covered the mat evenly.

6. Let the mat dry for 10 minutes or so, then thin your second color and sponge it on the mat.

7. Measure and pencil in the border, using the paper tape to mark the lines. Brush a base color around the border and let dry. Sponge on a contrasting color.

8. If desired, dampen a feather, dip it in some thinned paint, and stroke on lines of contrasting color. (See the gold and dark blue lines in the close-up.)

9. When the mats are completely dry, have them laminated.

SHOPPING TIPS

Sea sponges: bath shops and paint or craft stores that carry decorative painting supplies.

DESIGN: Sharon Tompkins

Making Paste Papers

Remember the squishy pleasure of finger painting? Paste papers bring it all back. They are remarkably simple to make; you have only to brush colored paste over a piece of paper, then wipe it off in interesting patterns. Once the paper is dry, you can use it to make the gifts on the following pages.

EST. TIME: 1½ HOURS (not counting chilling or drying)

MATERIALS

1 cup (237 ml) cornstarch

7½ cups (1¾ l) water

1½ teaspoons liquid dish detergent

Acrylic craft paint

1 teaspoon glycerin (optional)

A few drops oil of clove, oil of peppermint, or oil of cedar (optional)

Pieces of paper

Water

1. Make the paste a day ahead. To begin, place the cornstarch in the bowl and stir in 1 cup of the water.

2. Bring the remaining water to a boil. Gradually add the hot water to the cornstarch, beating constantly with the mixer. Make sure the mixture is smooth and free of lumps.

3. Blend in the dish detergent and (if desired) the glycerin. Both help to keep the paste smooth and pliable.

4. If desired, blend in one of the aromatic oils. They are deterrents to insects, who may otherwise consider the cornstarch lunch.

5. Cover the paste and store in a cool place overnight; it will thicken somewhat as it sits. The next day, remove the skin that will have formed on top. Stir the paste again, making sure it's lump-free. (If it's lumpy, resort to a blender.)

TOOLS

Large mixing bowl

Electric mixer

Wide, soft paint brush

Sponge

Drawing tools (comb, pencil eraser, cardboard, etc.)

Clothesline

Iron

6. Stir in the acrylic paint, starting with about 1 teaspoon and adding more until you are pleased with the color. The paste will look somewhat lighter on the paper than in the bowl.

THE PAPER

Pour water into a sink or flat pan and place the paper in it for a moment, to relax it. Remove the paper, place it on a flat surface, and sponge some of the water off it, working from the center to the edges. It should be perfectly flat and damp, rather than sopping.

THE PAINTING

Using a wide paint brush, apply an even coat of colored paste to the damp paper. Then draw your designs in the paint, using whatever implements are at hand: your finger, a pencil eraser, a fat-toothed comb, a small spackle knife, paint brushes of various widths, or a long, thin piece of cardboard.

Dry the finished papers on a clothesline or a rack. When dry, iron them on the wrong side to flatten them.

RECIPE: Mimi Schleicher

Mini Legal Pad

*t*housands of people cannot think, list, or plan without a junior legal pad. Decorative paper can turn this everyday necessity into a memorable gift.

EST. TIME: 2 HOURS

MATERIALS

Junior legal pad, usually about 8 by 5 inches (20.5 x 12.5 cm)

Paste paper (see page 64) or other decorative paper

White craft glue

Pencil

Raffia

TOOLS

Scissors

Ruler

1. Cut a piece of paste paper the same size as the strip of binding at the top of the legal pad. Glue the paper over the binding.

2. Cut a piece of paste paper exactly as wide as, and 4 inches (10 cm) longer than, the legal pad. Turn under about 1 inch (2.5 cm) on one end and glue the fold closed. Position the folded edge even with the bottom of the pad.

Wrap the paper over the top of the pad and glue it to the back. The paper will extend about 3 inches (7.5 cm) down the back.

3. Cut a strip of paper 1¼ inches (3 cm) wide and as long as the pencil. Spread glue on the wrong side of the paper, wrap it around the pencil, and press in place.

4. Tie the pencil to the pad with raffia.

DESIGN: Patty Schleicher

Simple Sewn Books

*b*lank books with classy covers are irresistible invitations to note, jot, or scribble. Portable journals and pocket-sized notebooks make splendid stocking stuffers.

EST. TIME: ½ HOUR

MATERIALS

Sheets of blank paper

Paste paper (see page 64) or other decorative paper

Heavy thread

TOOLS

Ruler

Pencil

Awl or ice pick

Very large needle

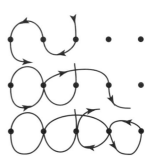

Figure 1

2. Place the sheets of paper in a carefully aligned stack. Lay the paste paper on top, right side up.

3. Measure to find the center of the stack—the future spine of the book—and mark it lightly in pencil. Make five dots down the spine, spacing them equally.

4. At each dot, punch a hole through all the layers.

5. Thread the needle and knot the thread. Starting on the inside of the book at the center hole, sew the book together, following the pattern in Figure 1. Tie the two thread ends together and trim the tails to about 1 inch (2.5 cm).

6. Fold the book in half along its spine.

DESIGN: Mimi Schleicher

1. Decide what size you want the book to be, and cut eight to 12 pieces of blank writing paper that size. Cut a piece of paste paper the same size. (If you want flaps on your cover, make the paste paper wider, so you can fold the ends under.)

Bookmarks

*n*o need to waste the scraps of paste paper left over from other projects. Bookmarks make great stocking stuffers.

EST. TIME: ¼ HOUR

MATERIALS

    Paste paper (see page 64) or other decorative paper

    Heavy paper or posterboard

    White craft glue

TOOLS

    Scissors

1. Cut strips of decorative paper and somewhat larger strips of heavier paper for the backing.

2. Glue the former to the latter.

3. If desired, take the bookmarks to your local office supply store or quick-print shop and have them laminated.

Origami Boxes

*t*hese paper boxes are remarkably sturdy. Treated halfway decently, they'll last for years. The boxes can be any size you like; just cut the paper for the lid ¼ inch (6 mm) larger than the paper for the bottom. For practice, cut an 8-inch (20.5 cm) lid and a 7¾-inch (20 cm) bottom from scrap paper.

EST. TIME: ½ HOUR per box

MATERIALS

Paste paper (page 64) or other decorative paper

Double-sided transparent tape

TOOLS

Pencil

Ruler

Scissors

1. On the wrong side of the paper square, draw light pencil lines between opposite corners, using the ruler for accuracy. See Figure 1.

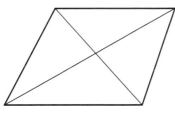

Figure 1

2. Fold two opposite corners into the center. See Figure 2. Lay the pencil or ruler flat over the fold and pull the ruler over the fold,

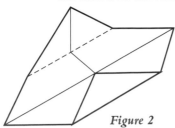

Figure 2

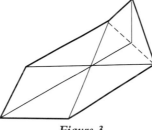

Figure 3

to make a sharp crease. Do the same for subsequent folds.

3. Now fold in the other two corners, making a smaller square. See Figure 3.

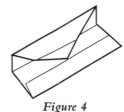

Figure 4

4. Fold one side of the square to the center. Then fold the other side to the center. See Figure 4.

Figure 5

5. Open the last two folds. Now fold the other two sides to the center in the same way. See Figure 5.

DESIGN: Mimi Schleicher

6. Open the last two folds; you've now got a square with creases. Using the scissors, make four cuts in the creases as shown. See Figure 6.

cut

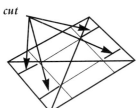

Figure 6

7. Unfold the long middle piece. See Figure 7.

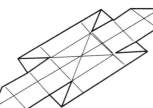

Figure 7

8. Lift the other two sides upright and unfold their outermost folds, to form a box. See Figure 8.

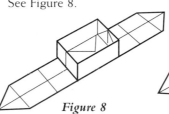

Figure 8

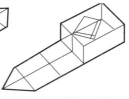

Figure 9

9. With the double-sided tape, make an X across the bottom of the box. Bring one of the long pointed ends over the side of the box and tuck the end into the bottom. Smooth it down so it forms a seal. See Figure 9.

10. Repeat for other long end. See Figure 10.

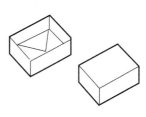

Figure 10

EASY PAINTING

Painting is too much fun to leave to people who know what they're doing. The rest of us should join right in.

You don't have to draw well (or even draw at all). A nod in the direction of an image—or no image at all—will do fine. Learn to use the terms *primitive* and *folk art* with authority. Later, throw in *stylized*. (That means the shrimp that's painted on the tablecloth isn't supposed to be anatomically correct.)

You need only a few supplies and materials.

FAUX PAINTING SUPPLIES

Plain wood and terra cotta can be made into exciting surfaces with faux painting. Now that it's wildly popular, *crackle glaze* and *faux finishing glaze* are available in craft shops, home improvement stores, and up-scale paint stores. Look for *universal tints* in a store that sells house paint. Used to create custom colors, these easy-to-mix tints come in standard artist's colors for a fraction of the cost of artist's oils. (They're sold by the ounce; take your own squirt bottles.) You'll find the *sea sponges* beloved by faux painters in bath shops.

GILDING SUPPLIES

In some cases, gilding the lily is actually a good idea. If you want to "paint" with gold, look in craft stores. Paper-thin sheets of *gold leaf* come in little booklets. *Gold size* or *adhesive size* is also there; it's the "glue" used to hold the leaf on the object.

FABRIC PAINT

Fabric paint is available in craft stores and craft departments of discount marts. Most fabric paints work only with natural fibers—for example, cotton, rayon, and linen. Check the label to make sure the paint is compatible with your fabric. Most fabric paints must be heat set with an iron; follow the package instructions.

Use a water-soluble fabric pen to do your outlining or sketching on fabric; you can remove the marks later with a damp cloth or even a wet finger. Avoid pens with ink that automatically disappears; it may disappear before you're ready.

Painted Candles

*t*hese elegant Christmas candles started out as inexpensive white tapers. A quick paint job made them special.

EST. TIME: ½ HOUR (not counting drying time)

MATERIALS

White or cream-colored candles

Gold spray paint

Red acrylic paint

Gold leaf paint (optional)

TOOLS

Sponge

Scissors

Paper plate

Paper towel

Paint brush (optional)

Sheila Schulz

1. Spray the candles with gold spray paint. Let dry.

2. Cut a small piece of sponge, about 1 inch (2.5 cm) square. Dampen it and wring out excess water.

3. Pour a little red paint onto a paper plate. Sponge-paint the candle in red, covering it uniformly. Let dry.

4. For extra glitter, accent the candles with sponged lines of gold leaf paint.

CAUTION:

Some paints (especially oil-based ones) are flammable. For safety's sake, candles painted with them should not be burned, but used only for decoration. (Char the wicks before you paint the candles.)

Gilded Frame

*a*nyone with pictures or mirrors to hang will be delighted with this handsome frame. Although it's covered with gold leaf, its clean lines and gorgeous sheen will be at home with any style, from formal to casual. Gilding supplies are available at most craft stores.

DESIGN: Sharon Tompkins

EST. TIME: 2 HOURS (not counting drying times)

MATERIALS

Water-based (acrylic) primer

Red or yellow semigloss latex paint

Water-based gold size

Talcum powder

1 book dutch metal imitation gold leaf

Walnut or mahogany stain-varnish

TOOLS

Fine-grit sandpaper

1- or 2-inch (2.5 or 5 cm) latex brush

Soft sable brush

Cotton wool

Soft rag

1. Brush acrylic primer over the entire frame, front and back. Allow to dry.

2. Paint the frame (front and back) with red or yellow paint and allow to dry. (A little of this base coat will show through the gold leaf. A red base coat will produce a darker, richer gold; a yellow base will produce a brighter tone. The frame in the photo has a red base.)

3. Sand the frame lightly. Apply a second base coat and allow to dry.

4. Paint the front of the frame with the gold size. Allow it to dry until tacky.

5. Dust your hands with talcum powder and lay a single sheet of gold leaf on the frame. Tap it down with the bristles of the sable brush. Working leaf by leaf, cover the entire frame. Then tap down the entire surface.

6. Allow the frame to sit for about 1 hour. Then brush off as much excess gold leaf as possible.

7. Dampen a piece of cotton wool with hot water and rub it over the frame, removing any remaining excess leaf. Allow to dry overnight.

8. Brush on walnut or mahogany stain varnish. With the soft rag, wipe off the high spots, allowing the recessed areas to remain dark.

Glorious Glass Plates

*S*ince all the paint and gold leaf are on the back of these elegant plates, they can be used as serving pieces or as the ultimate dining experience.

EST. TIME: 1½ HOURS (not counting drying time)

MATERIALS

Glass plates

Acrylic craft paints

Paper towels

Gold size

Gold leaf

Acrylic sealer or polyurethane spray

TOOLS

Scrap of sea sponge

Small plastic lid

Sponge brush

Combing tool (see note)

½-inch (1.5 cm) soft bristle brush

Small lint-free cloth

Cotton balls

Razor blade

1. Wash the plates well in warm, soapy water, being sure to remove all traces of those irritating gummed labels. Dry well.

2. To paint the sponged areas, dampen the sea sponge with water and wring out excess moisture. Pour a small amount of paint into the plastic lid. Lightly dab the sponge into the paint, then blot it on a paper towel to remove excess paint. Press the sponge onto the back of the plate in a random pattern, applying as much paint as you like. (Keep in mind that a layer of gold leaf will be applied on top of the paint and will be visible wherever there is no paint.) Allow the paint to dry at least 4 hours. If you want to use more than one color of paint, allow each coat to dry before applying the next.

3. To make the combed pattern shown on the rim of the green plate, first brush an even coat of paint onto the back of the plate, using the sponge brush. Drag the combing tool through the wet paint, scraping away the paint in a wavy, straight, or zigzag pattern. If you don't like the design, wash the paint off, apply another coat, and start again. Allow to dry completely.

4. Brush a uniform coat of adhesive size over

DESIGN: Terry Taylor

the back of the plate, using a soft brush. Allow to dry 30 minutes, or until tacky.

5. Lay a sheet of gold leaf on the size and lightly pat it in place. Working leaf by leaf, cover the back of the plate.

6. Place the cotton balls in the center of the cloth and bring the corners together, to form a padded ball. Use the ball to smooth the composition leaf into place. If there are large areas where the leaf did not adhere, apply more size and more leaf.

7. Check the edges of the plate for any wandering composition leaf. If any stuck there, scrape it off with the razor blade.

8. Allow the plate to dry overnight, or at least 4 hours.

9. When the plates are completely dry, spray their backs with the sealer. Allow to dry, then apply a second coat.

NOTE: Combing tools are available at most craft stores. If you can't find one, make your own by cutting evenly spaced notches on one edge of a piece of cardboard, using pinking shears or ordinary scissors and a careful hand.

Polka Dot Lamp

*t*urn an old lamp (or a boring new one) into an upbeat accessory with spray paint and a paint pen.

EST. TIME: 1 HOUR (not counting drying time)

MATERIALS

Lamp

Lamp shade

White acrylic enamel spray paint

Black and white paint pens

1. Spray the lamp base white. Allow to dry.

2. Add polka dots with the black paint pen, using any pattern you like. Follow the architecture of the lamp when deciding where to cluster the dots.

3. Add rows of white dots around the shade. (If you end up buying a new shade in the desired shape and color, take the lamp with you to check the fit.)

DESIGN: Ellen Zahorec

Child's Rocking Chair

a chair your own size with your own name on it—what child would not be delighted and instantly territorial? Buy a new chair or an old one that's structurally sound, then paint it any way you like (as long as you include the name).

EST. TIME: new chair, 4 HOURS; old chair, 8 HOURS.

MATERIALS

Rocking chair

Furniture stripper

Water-based primer

Acrylic paints in assorted colors

TOOLS

Sandpaper

Paint brushes in various sizes

1. If the chair is old, strip off the paint or finish, following the manufacturer's instructions. Allow to dry.

2. Sand the chair until smooth.

3. Brush the chair with a coat of primer and allow to dry.

4. Paint the base coats on the chair. Let its construction suggest color placement—one color for the rungs, another for the rockers, and so on. Allow to dry.

4. Add embellishments in contrasting colors—simple polka dots, perhaps a stenciled house, your idea of a sleeping cat.

5. Paint the child's name on the back of the chair. (This is *very* important.) Alphabet stencils from a discount mart make it easy, or you can simply paint the letters freehand.

Celestial Game Board

*e*ver feel like a pawn in a cosmic game of chess? Become a major player on this splendid game board. The fabric bag to hold the pieces is classy but optional.

EST. TIME: 5 HOURS (not counting drying time)

MATERIALS

Piece of plywood 34 x 16 x ⅝ inches (86.5 x 40.5 x 1.5 cm)

Acrylic craft paints in bright blue, dark gold, light gold, yellow, and bronze

Masking tape

Paper

24 wooden stars about 1½ inches (4 cm) in diameter (sold in craft stores)

3 yards (2.8 m) flat, blue braid trim ⅝ inch (1.5 cm) wide

Gold paint pen

Clear acrylic spray

Celestial fabric 7 by 24 inches (18 x 61 cm), optional

½ yard (45.5 cm) gold cord (optional)

TOOLS

2- or 3-inch (5 or 7.5 cm) paint brush

1-inch (2.5 cm) paint brush

½-inch (1.5 cm) paint brush

Pencil

Toothbrush

Metal ruler

Craft knife

Sewing machine (optional)

Glue gun

1. Paint both sides and all edges of the board blue. Let dry.

2. Tape paper over the outer 10 inches (25 cm) of each end of the board. With the masking tape, cover 1 inch (2.5 cm) at the top and 1 inch at the bottom of the open area. You should now have an unmasked opening 14 inches (35.5 cm) square.

3. Sketch the swirling starry areas on the paper at each end and cut out those areas. See Figure 1.

4. Pour a little dark gold paint into a shallow container and dilute it slightly with water. Dip the toothbrush in the paint, hold the brush over the board, and run your fingers across the bristles to splatter the board with dots of paint. (This will be gloriously messy; wear old clothes and use lots of newspapers.) Splatter lightly in the checkerboard area, heavily on the starry ends. Then splatter with a little light gold for highlights. Allow paint to dry, then remove tape and paper.

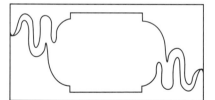

Figure 1

DESIGN: Kim Tibbals

Photocopy sun and moon at 500%.

5. While the board dries, paint 12 stars light gold and 12 bronze. Cover both sides and all edges.

6. Mask the board again in the same way, covering the outer 10 inches at each end, 1 inch at the top, and 1 inch at the bottom. Cover the entire 14-inch-square opening with strips of masking tape. Using a ruler or yardstick, mark off the grid pattern, drawing 64 ¾-inch (2 cm) squares. With the craft knife and the ruler, cut along all lines, including the outermost ones. Carefully lift the tape from alternating squares and splatter-paint the exposed areas with light gold, covering fairly thickly. Allow to dry and remove the mask.

7. While the board dries, make the bag for the checkers, if you plan to. Fold the fabric in half lengthwise, right sides together. Stitch one end and both long sides together, using a ½-inch (1.5 cm) seam. On the open end, fold 2½ inches (6.5 cm) to the wrong side and stitch along the lower edge.

Turn the bag right side out and press. Tack (hand-sew) the center of the gold cording to one edge of the bag, 2½ inches down from the top. Knot the ends of the cording.

8. Use a photocopier to enlarge the patterns for sun, moon, and stars. Trace them onto the board. (Or simply sketch them by hand.)

9. Paint the sun and moon faces yellow. Paint the large sun rays light gold and the small rays bronze. Paint the stars gold, light gold, and bronze. Outline the moon, sun, and all facial features with the gold paint pen. Also outline the playing area of the checkerboard, leaving the starry areas unlined to flow into space.

10. Cover both front and back of the board with acrylic sealer.

11. With the glue gun, glue the braid trim around the outside edges of the board.

Tortoiseshell Candlesticks

a beat-up pair of wooden candlesticks—a flea market find—
became a handsome present with an easy-to-apply finish.

EST. TIME: 1½ HOURS (not counting drying time)

MATERIALS

Wooden candlesticks

Gold spray paint

Oil-based faux finishing glaze

Universal tints or artists' oil paints in black, brown,
and burnt sienna

Paint thinner

Clear semigloss spray sealer

TOOLS

150-grit sandpaper

220-grit sandpaper

Small china bristle paint brushes

Soft badger blending brush or very soft paint brush

1. Using the coarse sandpaper, sand the candlesticks so the paint will adhere.

2. Spray the candlesticks with two even coats of gold spray paint, allowing them to dry between coats. Make sure they're completely dry.

3. Make a black glaze by mixing a drop of black tint into a tablespoon of finishing glaze. Make a brown glaze and a burnt sienna glaze in a similar way.

4. Brush a layer of clear glaze over the entire candlestick.

5. While the clear glaze is still wet, dip your brush into the black glaze and apply strips of color, going in the same direction. Do the same with the brown and the burnt sienna glazes. Work quickly and keep all the glazes wet.

DESIGN: Sheila Schulz

6. With the badger blender or soft paint brush, blend the colors into each other, keeping a light touch. Work in all directions on the first wipe, but all in one direction on the final wipe. (Tortoiseshell is directional.)

7. If you aren't pleased with the results as you work, simply wipe the glazes off with paint thinner and begin again.

8. Finish with several coats of clear sealer, allowing each coat to dry before another is added.

Rolled Beeswax Candles

*C*andlesticks are nothing without candles, and these classy tapers are five-minute projects. Sheets of beeswax in various colors and spools of wicking are available at well-stocked craft stores. Store the candles at room temperature out of direct sunlight.

EST. TIME: 10 MINUTES

MATERIALS

Sheet of beeswax

Wick

TOOLS

Sharp craft knife

Metal ruler (optional)

1. Bring the wax sheets to warm room temperature: 75° to 80° F (23° to 26° C). If they're too cool, the sheets will be brittle and hard to roll.

2. Cut a wick 1 inch (2.5 cm) longer than the candle will be tall. Lay it along one edge of the wax sheet, with the extra length at the top. See Figure 1.

3. Carefully fold about ¼ inch (6 mm) of wax over the wick and gently mash it down.

4. Roll up the candle, keeping it as tightly rolled as possible without mashing the honeycomb pattern. If you need more than one sheet, butt the second up against the first, or overlap them and press them together into the thickness of a single sheet.

5. When the candle is as thick as you want, cut off the remaining beeswax sheet, using the ruler as a straight-edge if desired. Gently press the cut edge into the body of the candle.

Figure 1

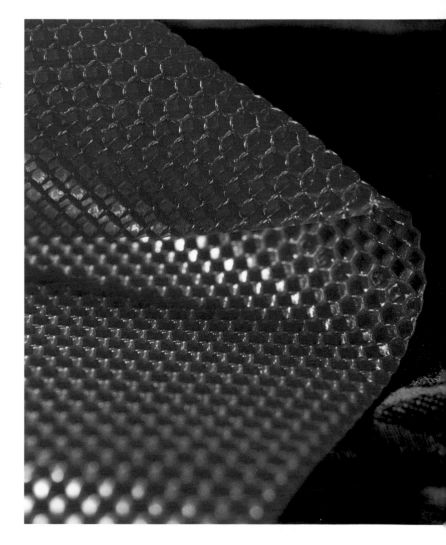

Painted Flower Pots

With their striking resemblance to semiprecious stones, these gorgeous pots will earn you enough points to last until spring. Add a potted plant or some easy-care silk flowers if you like.

EST. TIME: ½ HOUR (not counting drying time)

MATERIALS

Malachite (Green) Pot

Clay pot, any size

Pale teal latex or craft acrylic paint

Dark green latex or acrylic paint

Water-base glazing liquid

Satin varnish spray

TOOLS

1-inch (2.5 cm) latex or artist's brush

Thin cardboard

Small artist's brush

COLOR SUBSTITUTIONS

Lapis Lazuli (Blue) Pot

Base coat: Pale blue latex paint

Glaze: Dark blue latex paint

Interior: Dark rust latex paint

Coral Pot

Base coat: Off-white latex paint

Glazes: Burgundy, dark rust, gold, brown, and black latex paints

Interior: Medium blue latex paint

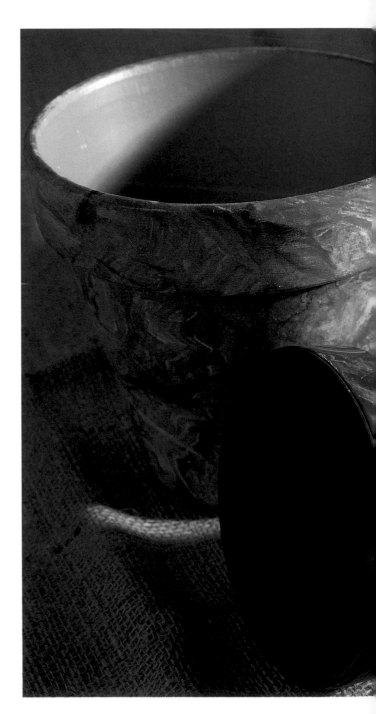

1. With the 1-inch brush, paint the pot inside and out with two base coats of teal paint. Allow each coat to dry.

2. Mix dark green paint, glazing liquid, and water, using about a 4:4:2 ratio. (For this project, use 2 ounces of paint, 2 ounces of glazing liquid, and 1 ounce of water; or 60 ml, 60 ml, and 30 ml.) Paint the mixture on the pot, covering it about one-third of the way around, from top to bottom.

3. Tear off a piece of cardboard 1 to 2 inches (2.5 to 5 cm) long and about ½ inch (1.5 cm) wide, and drag it through the wet glaze in curves and circles, jiggling it as you go.

4. Repeat with another one-third of the pot, then with the final third.

5. Add some darker accents, using the glaze-latex mixture and the artist's brush to spatter, dab, or streak within the broad bands of color. Allow the pot to dry.

6. Spray the pot with two coats of varnish to protect the finish, allowing it to dry after each coat.

7. Paint the inside of the pot with a contrasting color or with a final coat of base coat.

DESIGN: Sharon Tompkins

Painted Wooden Box

With simple sponge painting, a plain box becomes a one-of-a-kind present. Geometric shapes work well and are easy to apply.

DESIGN: Sharon Tompkins

EST. TIME: 1½ HOURS (not counting drying time)

MATERIALS

White acrylic primer

White latex semigloss paint

Pastel blue latex paint

Water-based glazing liquid

Pink latex paint

Satin varnish spray

TOOLS

2-inch (5 cm) latex paint brush

Natural sea sponge

Ruler or straight-edge

1-inch (2.5 cm) paper tape (or other non-tacky tape)

Pencil

Long, narrow artist's brush

1. Paint the box with the primer. Allow to dry.

2. Apply two coats of white semigloss paint, allowing each one to dry.

3. Mix equal parts of blue paint, glazing liquid, and water. Brush the mixture over the box top. Dampen the sponge and press it into the wet paint to create the sponged texture. Allow to dry.

4. With the ruler and pencil, find and mark the center of each side of the lid. Connect the centers with diagonal strips of tape; the inner edges of the tape should meet to form a point. You will paint lines along each edge of the tape.

5. Make a white glaze by mixing white paint, glazing liquid, and water in equal proportions. Make a pink glaze in the same way.

6. Dip the dampened sponge in the white glaze and apply it to the lid, inside the taped lines. Sponge pink glaze on the corners.

7. Tape stripes on the sides of the box and sponge in the colors. If desired, tape a diamond on opposite sides and paint as shown.

8. Using a felt-tip marker or latex paint and the narrow artist's brush, outline the shapes in solid colors.

9. After the paint is completely dry, apply two coats of satin varnish.

Stenciled Lamp

*W*ith stars that seem to glow when the light is on, this stenciled and spray-painted lamp is great for a child's room. Any simple shape would work as well.

EST. TIME: 1½ HOURS (not counting drying time)

MATERIALS

Clear shelf paper with peel-off backing

Lamp and shade

Masking tape

Acrylic enamel spray paint

Gold paint marker

TOOLS

Scissors

1. Working freehand and carefree, cut out stars from the clear shelf paper, cutting as many as you want to use on the shade. (They should not be perfect, so restrain the impulse to be too good.) For the bottom border, make some "negative" stars—that is, cut out a rectangle of paper, then cut a star shape out of the center of the rectangle.

2. Peel off the backing of each star and press the star onto the shade.

3. Tape the lamp's metal fixture and cord, at least near the base. Holding the can 2 feet (61 cm) from the shade at first, lightly spray the shade with paint; a heavy coat will drip. For more intense color, let the paint dry for a few minutes, then spray lightly again. When the shade is completely dry, peel off the stencils.

4. Spray paint the lamp base. Allow to dry.

5. Using the gold paint marker, add a decorative edging around the base, the top and bottom of the shade, and the border of negative stars.

Crackle Finish Platter

Unfinished wooden platters make fine canvases and, eventually, fine presents. Depending on their size, they can serve as platters or as charger plates to set under the dinner plates.

EST. TIME: 1½ HOURS (not counting drying time)

MATERIALS

Unfinished wooden platter or charger plate

Latex semi-gloss paint in a dark color (red, black, or green)

Latex semi-gloss paint in white or cream

Crackle glaze

Oil-based faux finishing liquid glaze

Universal tint or artist's oil paint in raw umber

Paint thinner

Liquid gold leaf paint (optional)

Spray enamel in color of your choice (for back of platter)

Clear varnish spray

TOOLS

0000 steel wool

Several 2-inch (5 cm) paint brushes

Small sponge

Plastic containers or tin cans for mixing glaze

1. With the steel wool, lightly sand the platter.

2. Apply one or two coats of the darker latex paint and allow to dry thoroughly.

3. Brush a thin layer of crackle glaze over the platter, working against the grain of the wood. Allow to dry for about 1 hour.

4. Using a good paint brush, apply the white or cream-colored latex paint. Get enough paint on your brush so that you don't have to paint the same area more than once (which will peel off the crackle glaze). On this paint layer, apply the paint with the grain (opposite the crackle). Allow to dry. The crackle effect should appear immediately. The thicker the coat of paint, the larger the crackles. Your darker color will show through the cracks.

5. When the platter is completely dry, sand it lightly with the steel wool.

6. Mix a drop or two of the raw umber colorant into 1 or 2 tablespoons of faux finishing glaze. Brush this glaze on the platter, then wipe it off with a rag, for an aged look.

7. When the platter is completely dry, spray-paint the back in the color of your choice. Allow to dry.

8. With the sponge, paint a band of gold leaf paint around the outside edge of the plate. Allow to dry.

9. Spray the platter with clear varnish or sealer.

VARIATION

The platter on the second level has a white base coat, rather than a dark one. The second coat—a medium beige—was applied very thickly, to produce large cracks. The platter is finished with light brown furniture wax, rather than spray varnish.

Faux Leather Platter

MATERIALS

Unfinished wooden platter or charger plate

Semi-gloss spray enamel in tan, black, and red

Wallpaper paste

Tissue paper

Furniture wax (not polish)

Gold leaf paint

TOOLS

Fine-grit sandpaper

Paint brushes

0000 steel wool

Small sponge

1. Sand the platter lightly with the sandpaper.

2. Spray the platter with two coats of tan paint, allowing each coat to dry. Paint the back black.

3. Spread a thin layer of wallpaper paste over the platter, covering all the way out to the edges. While the paste is still wet, lay a sheet of tissue paper on the platter. With your hands, move the tissue around until you have as much leather texture as you want. Smooth out the tissue around the edges of the platter. Allow to dry completely.

4. Lightly sand the outer edge of the platter so that the edges are smooth and there is no loose tissue.

5. Spray on a very thin coat of red paint. While the red is still a bit wet, spray on a thin layer of black. Allow to dry very thoroughly.

6. Buff the platter with the steel wool, to give the leather texture more definition.

7. Coat the platter with furniture wax, allow to dry, then buff again with steel wool.

8. Dip the corner of the sponge into the gold paint and outline the edge of the platter.

DESIGN: Sheila Schulz

Brassy Stamped Hat

*t*urn an inexpensive canvas hat into a fiercely guarded possession that will not be lent out, no matter how sweetly the request is phrased.

EST. TIME: 1 HOUR

MATERIALS

Black canvas hat

Metallic fabric paints in gold, silver, and brass

TOOLS

Paint brush

Plastic or heavy paper plate

Spools from thread

Plastic bottle caps

Pencil eraser

1. Look around for any-thing that will print a circle (see list above for examples).

2. Brush a little paint of each color on the plate. Dab your object into the paint and press it onto the rim of the hat.

3. Continue around the brim until it's covered. Add a ring of circles on the crown. Vary the colors, the objects, and the number of repeats. Make circles within circles.

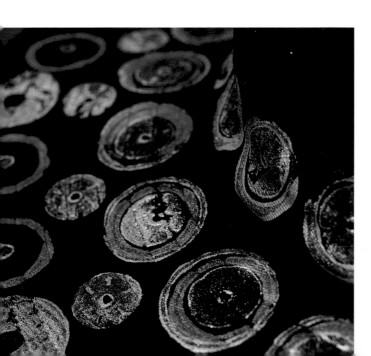

DESIGN: Ellen Zahorec

Bouillabaisse Tablecloth and Napkins

*t*he stylized clams, shrimp, and tomatoes on these contemporary-looking table linens are brushed on with fabric paint. Look closely before you quail. The tomato is just a squashed circle with a few green leaves. The clam is a triangle with one rounded side. The jaunty shrimp is just a tube with a few loops on one end.

EST. TIME: 4 HOURS (not counting drying time)

MATERIALS

    100% cotton tablecloth and napkins

    Fabric paints in light green, yellow, tomato red, dark green, white, and black

TOOLS

    Water-soluble fabric marker

    Ruler or tape measure

    Paint brushes in various widths

    Fine-tipped black fabric marker or pipette bottle and black paint

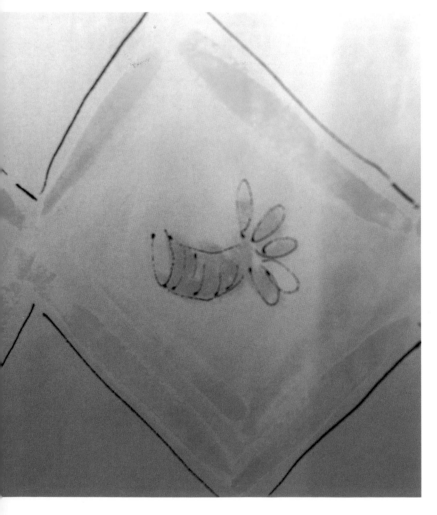

1. Wash and dry the tablecloth and napkins, to remove any sizing the manufacturer may have added. Sizing will repel the paint. Iron the linens for a wrinkle-free canvas.

2. Lay the tablecloth flat. Using the tape measure and the water-soluble fabric marker, outline the basic diamond border around the tablecloth. While the design shouldn't be perfectly regular, it shouldn't crawl up and down the side of the cloth, either.

3. Paint the green border around the cloth. Try to keep a free spirit. This isn't brain surgery. Variations in the brush strokes will add charm, not embarrassment. Don't use too much paint on your brush—the strokes should be semidry, rather than gloppy, and some of the fabric should show through. Allow the paint to dry. Paint a free-form green line around half the napkins, as a border.

4. Paint the yellow border of the tablecloth as you did the green. Paint a free-form yellow line around the remaining napkins. Let dry.

5. Using the fabric marker, outline the basic shapes of the tomatoes and seafood, one item to a diamond. Place them in whatever order you like.

6. Working with the dark green, then the red, paint the toma-

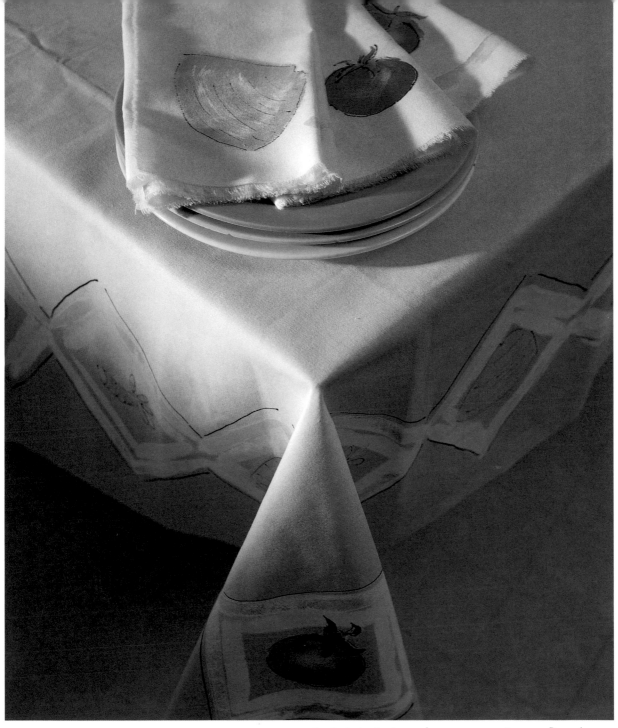

DESIGN: L o v e e t a   B a k e r

toes, using a fairly dry brush. Try not to be perfect. Allow each color to dry before adding the next.

7. Mix the paint for the seafood: white, yellow, and a tiny bit of red. Paint the shrimp and clams. Allow to dry completely.

8. Using the white paint, add highlights to the tomatoes and clams, using the photo as a guide (or striking out on your own). Allow to dry.

9. Finally, add the fine black lines that outline the diamonds and the seafood. If you're familiar with a pipette bottle (available at art supply stores) or want to become so, it's a great tool for the job. Otherwise, use a fine-tipped black fabric marker.

Stenciled Napkins

*b*ecause stenciling is such a popular craft, most craft stores or craft departments in discount marts carry stencil sheets—thin pieces of clear acrylic ready to be cut out—as well as stubby, flat-bottomed stenciling brushes.

EST. TIME: 4–6 HOURS

MATERIALS

Paper

Acrylic stencil sheets

Masking tape

Cardboard or foam core

Cotton napkins

Fabric paint

Paper towels

TOOL

Sharp craft knife

Acrylic marker

Iron

Stencil brushes

Small bowls or paper plates

1. On a piece of paper, draw your design. If you like, photocopy the pattern given, enlarging it as desired on the copier. Decide what colors will go where.

2. You'll need to cut (and paint) a separate stencil for each color—one for all the green in the design, another for all the red, and so on. To make sure that the colors are reasonably positioned on the finished napkin—that the green leaves are actually near the red twigs, for example—draw heavy dots on two opposite corners of a stencil sheet, using a pen that will mark on acrylic. Lay each remaining stencil sheet over the first and make the same dots in the same position. Lay a stencil sheet on the napkin and make a couple of light pencil marks under the dots. Use these dots to position the stencils.

3. Lay a stencil sheet over the pattern and trace onto it all those areas that will be one color. Trace an additional stencil for each remaining color.

4. Using the craft knife, cut out all the areas on the stencils that you want to paint.

5. Iron the napkin and tape it flat to a piece of cardboard or foam core. Lay a stencil over it and tape it in place, aligning the dots.

6. Pour a little fabric paint in a bowl or

paper plate and dip the end of the brush into the paint. Dab the brush onto a paper towel, removing most of the paint; you'll be working with an almost dry brush. Lightly paint the open areas of the stencil, using an up-and-down dabbing motion, not a back-and-forth brush-ing motion. When all areas are painted, let dry for a few minutes. If you want more intense color, add another light coat of paint. Allow the paint to dry before removing the stencil. Otherwise, the paint will smudge.

8. Stencil the remaining napkins and the remaining colors. To overlap the drying times, work on differ-ent colors on different napkins; that way, they call all be drying at the same time.

9. Set the paint, accord-ing to package instructions.

Hand-Painted Shirt and Tie

*t*he paisley design in an old tie supplied the motif for this gift set. The designer simply painted over it with fabric paint pens, then repeated the pattern on the shirt's collar, pocket, and cuffs.

EST. TIME: 2 HOURS

MATERIALS

Paper

Shirt

Tie

TOOLS

Pencil

Enamel or acrylic paint pens in gold and silver

1. Sketch out your basic design on scrap paper and select the paint colors you prefer. (A white shirt and bright colors would produce quite a different look from the one shown here, as would a black shirt.)

2. Paint the design on the clothing.

Gold-Stamped Vest

When the silk fabric of this purchased vest absorbed most of the paint from her rubber stamp, the designer brushed on a few rectangles of color to provide a less absorbent surface, then stamped over the painted areas.

EST. TIME: 6 HOURS (including drying)

MATERIALS

Purchased vest

Acrylic fabric paints in gold, white, fuchsia, and green

TOOLS

Rubber stamp

1-inch or 1½-inch (2.5 or 4 cm) paint brush

1. Before starting on your purchased vest, it's a good idea to test the stamp and the paint on a scrap of similar fabric.

2. Pour a little gold paint in a flat dish, dip the stamp in it, and press the stamp onto the fabric. If you end up with too much paint on the vest, press the wet stamp on a paper towel or fabric scrap first, then onto the garment. Stamp as much of the vest as you like.

3. If the fabric absorbs too much of the paint—leaving only faint traces of color—incorporate painted areas into your design. Paint white rectangles and allow to dry. Then stamp in gold over the painted areas.

4. When the stamped rectangles are dry, thin a little fuchsia paint with water; thin some green also. Brush some painted areas with the fuchsia glaze, others with the green.

FAST FOOD

When we need a last-minute Christmas gift, the first thing we think of is food. It's fast, it's easy, and just about everyone loves to eat.

True, *everyone* brings gifts of food during the Christmas season. On the other hand, in less time than it takes to bake a loaf of cranberry bread, you can prepare savory, imaginative, even elegant food that won't be duplicated by anyone else in the neighborhood.

Herbal Oils

*O*live oil infused with the flavors of fresh herbs—guaranteed to delight any food lover. Dribble it over pasta and add a grating of fresh Parmesan for an instant dinner. Place a bowl of oil on the table, add fresh Parmesan, and serve it as a dipping sauce for Italian or French bread. Use it to saute fresh vegetables or to dress roasted ones. Combine it with vinegar for an instant salad dressing.

EST. TIME: ¼ HOUR

YOU WILL NEED

  Decorative bottle

  Fresh herbs

  Extra-virgin olive oil

1. Place the herbs in a clean bottle.

2. Fill the bottle with oil.

3. The oil should be stored in a cool, dark place for two weeks before it's used, to allow the flavors to infuse into the oil. Subtract whatever stor-age time you've used up (if any) and note the remainder on the gift card.

4. Also note on the card: "At the end of two weeks, remove and discard the herbs. Stored on the shelf, the oil should be used within a month.

Stored in the refrigerator and brought to room temperature before using, it will last indefinitely."

A variety of herbs will have excellent results. Here are two well-tested favorites.

PROVENCE MEDLEY

Rosemary, basil, thyme, dried tomatoes, oregano, dill, pepper-corns, garlic clove

HOT PEPPER OIL

Cilantro, jalapeño peppers (cut length-wise), peppercorns, dried tomatoes, zest of 2 limes

DESIGN: Renée Garcia   103

Herbed Cheese

*P*arsley, basil, rosemary, chives—fresh herbs are handsome wrappings for the smooth cheese inside. Look in upscale supermarkets or specialty food stores for fresh herbs in midwinter.

EST. TIME: ½ HOUR plus chilling time

INGREDIENTS

- Plain goat cheese
- Fresh herbs
- Sweet red pepper
- Extra-virgin olive oil

1. Coarsely chop herbs and peppers and place them in small bowls.

2. Form balls of goat cheese, using a small ice cream scoop. Roll balls in coatings and chill.

3. Just before serving, drizzle with olive oil and garnish with whole stems of herbs.

Phyllo Puffs

*P*hyllo dough is instant pastry. Easy to work with and absolutely delicious, it's available in frozen packages at most supermarkets. Fill the thin, light sheets with either of the mixtures given, bake briefly, and delight anyone who really likes food.

EST. TIME: 45 MINUTES (not counting thawing)

Sago Blue Cheese Filling

Crumble this mild, tasty cheese into bits of manageable size.

Red Pepper and Artichoke Filling

1 small jar pimentos

1 can artichoke hearts

2 cups (237 ml) mayonnaise

2 to 3 cups (500 to 700 ml) grated Parmesan cheese

1 medium onion, coarsely chopped

Juice and zest of 1 lemon

Fresh or dried dill

Drain pimentos and artichoke hearts. Combine with remaining ingredients.

WORKING WITH PHYLLO

Phyllo dough consists of pliable, paper-thin layers of pastry. If you tear a sheet or two, fear not; there are more sheets in the package than you are going to use.

Thaw the phyllo according to the package instruction. To prevent the sheets from becoming dry and brittle, keep them covered with a damp towel when not actively working with them.

MAKING BUNDLES

Cut 4-inch (10 cm) squares through all layers of pastry. Peel off a layer of phyllo and brush it with melted butter. Cover it with a second layer and brush that with butter. Top with a third layer.

Place 1 tablespoon of filling in the center of the phyllo squares. Bring the corners together and squeeze the bundle together above the filling.

Place the bundles in muffin pans and bake in preheated oven at 375° F (190° C) until brown, about 5 to 7 minutes.

MAKING CUPS

Cut 2-inch (5 cm) squares through all layers of pastry. Brush with butter and layer as above. Place the squares in muffin tins and press them into the cups to shape them. Fill and bake until brown, about 5 to 7 minutes.

Red and Green Salsas

*t*raditional Christmas colors take untraditional form in this gift basket. In a season of endless sweets, picante snacks are a welcome change. Add tomato and blue corn chips for dipping.

EST. TIME: ¾ HOUR for both salsas

SALSA RIOJA

Since "fresh" wintertime tomatoes are often pale and wan, good-quality canned plum tomatoes make a better December salsa. Use one fresh tomato for texture.

1 medium tomato

6 canned plum tomatoes

4 green onions

1 clove garlic, minced

2 jalapeño peppers

4-ounce (115 g) can chopped green chiles

1 teaspoon olive oil

1 tablespoon lime juice

Salt to taste

¼ cup (59ml) tomato juice

¼ cup (20g) chopped cilantro

Chop the tomatoes and green onions. Mince the garlic and jalapeños. Stir in remaining ingredients.

YIELD: 1½ TO 2 CUPS

Salsa Verde

Vary the number of peppers to suit the intended receiver. In these recipes, the red salsa is considerably hotter than the green.

12 to 14 tomatillos

1 small onion, chopped

1 clove garlic, minced

1 serrano pepper, minced

2 tablespoons vegetable oil

$\frac{1}{4}$ teaspoon sugar

Salt to taste

$\frac{1}{4}$ cup (20 g) chopped cilantro

Remove the brown, papery husks from the tomatillos and simmer them 5 minutes, or until easily pierced with a fork. Drain and process briefly in a blender or food processor, until you have a coarse puree. Saute the onion, garlic, and pepper in the oil 5 to 10 minutes, or until onions are soft, and add to the puree. Stir in the sugar, salt, and cilantro.

Yield: 1 $\frac{1}{2}$ to 2 cups

Snack Basket

*i*nclude a healthful item or two among these sweet and savory snacks, just to allay those seasonal pangs of guilt.

EST. TIME: ½ HOUR

MATERIALS

> Yogurt-covered malt balls, pistachios, oriental rice snacks, salted almonds, mixed dried fruit, mini pretzels, honey-roasted peanuts, or other snacks
>
> Small brown paper bags
>
> Flat basket
>
> Ribbon
>
> Pinecones
>
> Gold spray paint (optional)

1. Weave a festive ribbon around the basket.

2. Fold over the tops of the paper bags and fill each one with a different snack.

3. Place the bags in the basket. If desired, add a few plain or gilded pinecones.

Jerked Spice Blend

*O*riginally a Jamaican concoction, "jerked" meats have become downright trendy. This hot and spicy seasoning also jazzes up chicken, fish, and vegetables.

EST. TIME: ¼ HOUR

INGREDIENTS

- 1 tablespoon onion flakes
- 1 tablespoon onion powder
- 1 tablespoon granulated garlic
- 2 teaspoons ground thyme
- 2 teaspoons salt
- 1 teaspoon ground allspice
- ¼ teaspoon ground cinnamon
- ¼ teaspoon ground nutmeg
- 2 teaspoons sugar
- 1 teaspoon coarsely ground black pepper
- 1 teaspoon cayenne pepper
- 2 teaspoons dried chives or green onions
- Dried parsley

Laurey Masterton

1. Layer the spices in a glass jar, alternating colors as desired.

2. Accompany the jar blend with the following directions: "Stir the spices well before using. Coat meat, chicken, or fish before roasting or grilling. For a flavorful dip for vegetables, mix to taste with yogurt or sour cream."

Smoked Trout Paté

*P*acked in a mini loaf pan or spooned into an attractive bowl, this delicate spread is a great gift during a season of constant entertaining. Smoked salmon substitutes well for the trout.

NEXT-TO-THE-LAST-MINUTE VERSION

EST. TIME: ½ HOUR (not counting chilling)

- 1 envelope unflavored gelatin
- ¼ cup (59 ml) cold water
- ½ cup (118 ml) boiling water
- ½ cup mayonnaise
- 1 tablespoon lemon juice
- Zest of 1 lemon
- 1 tablespoon coarsely chopped red onion
- 2 tablespoons finely chopped fresh dill
- 1 smoked trout fillet
- 1 cup (237 ml) heavy cream

1. In a large mixing bowl, soften the gelatin in the cold water. Stir in the boiling water and whisk the mixture slowly until the gelatin dissolves. Cool to room temperature.

2. Whisk in mayonnaise, lemon juice, lemon zest, onion, and dill. Refrigerate until mixture is thickened (about 15 minutes).

3. Skin the trout filet and break the fish into flakes. Blend the fish into the mayonnaise mixture.

4. Whip the cream until soft peaks form. Fold it into the trout mixture.

5. Spoon the paté into a mold. Refrigerate at least 4 hours.

6. Tell the recipient that the paté can be unmolded onto a serving plate, if desired.

YIELD: 2 OR 3 SMALL BREAD PANS.

SHOPPING TIP

Most well-stocked groceries carry fresh dill in the produce section. Unfortunately, dried dill just doesn't work well in this recipe.

THE-VERY-LAST-MINUTE VERSION

EST. TIME: ¼ HOUR (not counting chilling)

- 1 pound (.45 kg) cream cheese
- ⅓ cup (80 ml) sour cream
- 1 smoked trout fillet
- 1 tablespoon lemon juice
- Zest of 1 lemon
- 2 tablespoons fresh dill

1. Skin the fillet

2. Place all ingredients in a food processor. Mix by pulsing three or four times. (Do not overmix.) Spoon the mixture into a mold or a pretty bowl. (This version can't be unmolded.) Garnish, chill for at least 1 hour, and give away.

YIELD: 2 SMALL BREAD PANS

WIRE AND WOOD

As much as they differ from each other, wire and wood are alike in at least two ways. Both are remarkably versatile. They can be shaped into an enormous variety of presents to please even the most particular. And both are somewhat unexpected. When we think of handmade gifts, we don't usually think of wire and wood. A gift made from either will both surprise and please.

Spiral Bracelet

*t*hanks to widely available "memory wire"—coiled steel wire that remains coiled—there is no easier jewelry to make. Check bead stores and craft shops for the wire and the beads to put on it.

EST. TIME: ½ HOUR

MATERIALS

Memory wire

Large-holed beads

TOOLS

Wire cutters

Needle-nose pliers

1. Cut the wire to the length desired, depending on the number of coils you want in the bracelet.

2. String the beads onto the wire. Avoid beads with small holes—if you have to force one around the wire, use another bead—and avoid very long beads, which will distort the wire's curves.

3. Check that the beads lie next to each other well. Avoid large beads on adjacent coils that crowd each other and force the coils apart.

4. With the needle-nose pliers, form a loop in each end of the wire, to hold the beads on. Point the loop away from the arm.

Hoop Earrings

"enough earrings"—an alien, possibly subversive concept. Another pair is always welcome. Bead stores and well-stocked craft shops carry both the beads and the hoops to hold them.

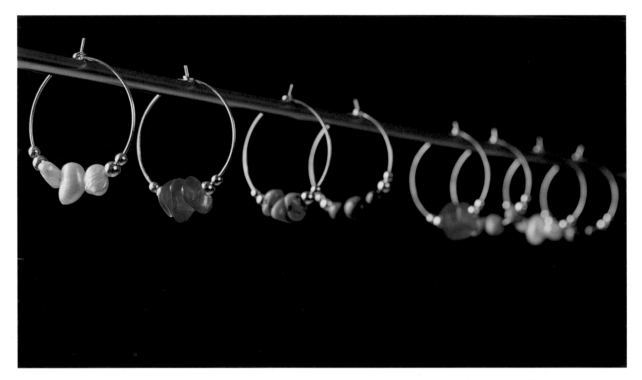

DESIGN: Lou Eremita

EST. TIME: 10 MINUTES

MATERIALS

Sterling silver ear hoops

Sterling silver beads

Beads or chips of your choice

1. The success of this simple design depends on the quality of the materials. Select sterling silver or gold-filled hoops and quality beads. Shown are freshwater pearls, amber chips, turquoise chips, and malachite beads, with sterling silver accent beads on each side.

2. String the beads on the hoops.

Drop Earrings

*F*or these earrings you'll need a few beads, a couple of head pins (straight pieces of wire with a flat head on one end to keep the beads from falling off), and a pair of ear wires or posts. All are available wherever beads are sold.

EST. TIME: ½ HOUR

MATERIALS

Beads

2 head pins

Pair of ear wires or posts

TOOLS

Wire cutters

Needle-nose pliers

1. Slip the beads onto the head pin, arranging them any way you like.

2. Cut the head pin off about ¼ inch (6 mm) above the beads.

3. Grasp the cut end of the head pin with the pliers and bend it into a loop. Leave the loop barely open.

4. Slip the loop of the head pin through the loop of the ear wire. Squeeze the pin's loop closed with the pliers.

DESIGN: Cindy Vandewart and Barbara Wright

Bead Necklace

*F*or an elegant string of beads, choose a few colors—in this case, russet, green, cream, and gold—and select beads in a variety of shapes and materials. Any store that sells beads will also carry beading needles and thread. Instead, you can use upholstery thread and any needle with an eye slim enough to go through your beads.

EST. TIME: 2 HOURS

MATERIALS

    Heavy thread

    Tape

    Beads

    Clear nail polish or bead glue

TOOLS

    2 needles

    Scissors

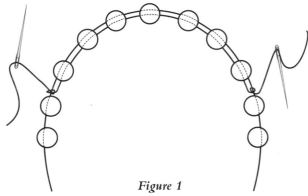

Figure 1

1. Cut a piece of thread twice the finished length of the necklace plus 1 yard (.9 m). For example, to make the 50-inch strand shown here, cut the thread 3¾ yards long (3.46 m). Note: A necklace must be at least 24 inches (61.5 cm) long to go over the head.

2. Thread on a needle. Double the thread but don't knot it. Tape the tails together temporally about 8 inches (20.5 cm) from the end.

3. String on the beads, alternating sizes, shapes, and colors.

4. When the beads are strung, untape the tails and string the second needle onto both of them. (You now have a needle on each end of the necklace.) Take each needle through three or four beads on the opposite end of the string. Tie each tail to the necklace between two beads, using a double knot. See Figure 1. Clip the thread ends and dab a little nail polish or bead cement on the knots.

Mini Skewers

With some silver wire and a few glass beads, you can make a set of hors d'oeuvre picks that will be someone's favorite gift. Silver wire is available in craft and bead stores. The higher the gauge, the thinner the wire.

EST. TIME: 2 HOURS for 4 skewers

MATERIALS

For each skewer:

4- to 6-inch (10.5-15.5 cm) length of 16-gauge silver wire, for the stem

12-inch (31 cm) length of 20-gauge silver wire, for the wrapping

Large-holed bead

TOOLS

Wire cutters

Hammer

Anvil (or a very hard, flat surface)

Needle-nose pliers

Metal file

1. Lay the piece of 16-gauge wire on the anvil and hammer one end of it relatively flat, to about half the wire's original thickness. The flattened area will extend above the bead. A flat area between ½ and 1½ inches long (1.5 to 4 cm) works well.

2. String the bead on the wire, pushing it up against the flattened section.

3. Use the pliers to make a decorative loop or bend in the center of the 20-gauge wire. Hold the loop against the bead, to check that the size and shape are reasonable. Lay the wire loop on the anvil and hammer it flat.

4. Place the loop against the bead. Wrap one end of the wire around the stem right above the bead. Wrap the other end around the stem right below the bead. Clip excess wire ends.

5. Lay the skewer on the anvil. Gently flatten the stem below the wrapped bead.

6. Use the file to grind the bottom of the skewer to a point.

Copper Napkin Rings

*t*hese striking napkin holders are simply pieces of heavy copper wire bent into shape. Sterling silver would also work well.

EST. TIME: ¼ HOUR per ring

MATERIALS

  16-gauge wire

TOOLS

  Wire cutters

  Needle-nose pliers

  Wooden dowel or other form

1. For each ring, cut a piece of wire about 15 inches (38 cm) long.

2. With the pliers, twist one end of the wire into a loop. Then grasp the loop across its full width with the pliers. Use your other hand to wrap the wire around the initial loop, creating a spiral. See Figure 1.

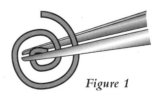

Figure 1

3. About ½ inch (1.5 cm) from the spiral, wrap the wire around anything large and solid enough to serve as a mold: a wooden dowel, a sturdy jar, a broom handle. Make as many twists as you like.

4. Make a spiral in the other end of the wire.

DESIGN: Virginia Wayne

CD Rack

*g*ive your friends a place to put all the CDs they're going to get for Christmas. This handy rack is essentially a box with shelves made of dowels. A slide moves over the dowels to prop up errant artists.

EST. TIME: 2 HOURS

MATERIALS

  8 feet of 1 x 6 board

  2 48-inch dowels ½ inch in diameter

  Paper

  6 #8 x 1¼ flathead wood screws

  3 feet of face trim

  #17 finishing nails

TOOLS

  Jigsaw or handsaw

  Pencil

  Power drill

  ½-inch brad point or forstner drill bit

  ⁹⁄₁₆ spade drill bit

  Sandpaper

1. Cut three pieces of 1 x 6 18 inches long. Rip (cut lengthwise) a piece for the back brace that is 14 inches long and 1¼ inches wide. (Alternatively, use a 14-inch length of 1 x 2 lumber for the back brace.) Cut six dowels 15 inches long.

2. Using Figure 1 as a guide, draw a full-size paper template for the sides. Lay the template on one of the 18-inch boards and draw circles to mark the holes

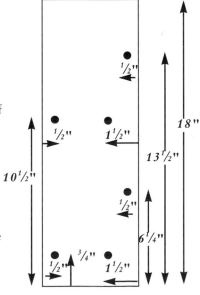

Figure 1

DESIGN: Craig Weis

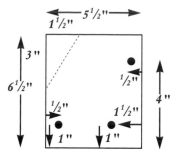

Figure 2

for the dowels. Reverse the template and mark another board, for the other side.

3. Tape the ½-inch drill bit so that the bottom of the tape is 1/4 inch from the tip of the bit. (This will discourage you from drilling too shallow or too deep.) Drill the holes ¼ inch deep, drilling as close to the center of each circle as you can.

4. Figure 2 indicates the dimensions for the slides, as well as the positions for the dowel holes. Using the bottom of the template you already cut, position the holes according to Figure 2 and drill them through with the ⁹⁄₁₆ bit. Saw off the top front corner of each slide as indicated. (The two slides are identical, not mirror images.)

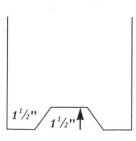

Figure 3

5. If desired, notch the bottom of each leg, as shown in Figure 3. Dry fit everything together: run the dowels through the slides and insert the dowels into the holes on each side. (Sanding the ends of the dowels will help them fit into the holes.) If the slides are sticking, drill out the holes a little more. Check the fit of the back brace. Trim or sand if needed.

6. With the parts dry-fitted, pre-drill holes for the screws. Lay the remaining 18-inch board across the top and mark where it crosses the sides. Drill four holes in the top—two where it crosses each side—positioning each hole 1 inch from the edge. See Figure 4.

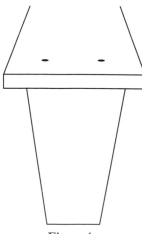

Figure 4

7. Drill a hole on each side 1 inch from the bottom and ¼ inch in from the back edge, for the back brace.

8. Sand all the parts.

9. Once you're happy with the fit, screw the top of the rack and the bottom brace into position.

10. Cut pieces of face trim to fit around the edges of the top and nail in place with finishing nails. If desired, miter the front corners at a 45° angle. See Figure 5.

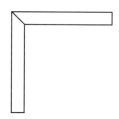

Figure 5

11. Seal the wood with polyurethane, or stain or paint it. (A too-heavy coat of paint may prevent the slide from moving freely over the dowels.)

NOTE: Metric equivalents are on page 128.

Bird Feeder

*O*ne of wintertime's great pleasures is watching the birds that cluster around a well-filled feeder. This simple-to-make model will help keep them fat and happy all winter long.

EST. TIME: 2 HOURS (not counting drying time)

MATERIALS

   4 feet of 1 x 8 board

   2-foot length of 1 x 4

   2 feet of base cap trim $\frac{7}{8}$ x $\frac{11}{16}$ inch

   3 x 3 or 2 x 2 hinge

   4d galvanized nails

   17 x 1-inch wire brads

   2 size 8 screw eyes

   2 yards of $\frac{1}{2}$-inch rope

TOOLS

   Saw

   Hammer

   Power drill with $\frac{1}{16}$, $\frac{5}{64}$, and $\frac{1}{2}$-inch bits

1. Cut the 1 x 8 board into the following lengths: 11 inches (for the lid); 8½ inches (for the front); 12 inches (for the back); and 6 inches (for the bottom). Saw the 1 x 4 into two 12-inch pieces (for the sides).

2. Measure and mark 10 inches up one edge of a side piece. Draw a line from that mark to the top of the other edge. Cut along the line, to angle the top of the side at about 25°. See Figure 1. Repeat for other side.

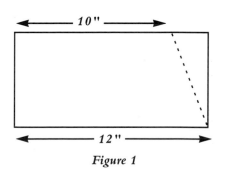

Figure 1

DESIGN: Craig Weis

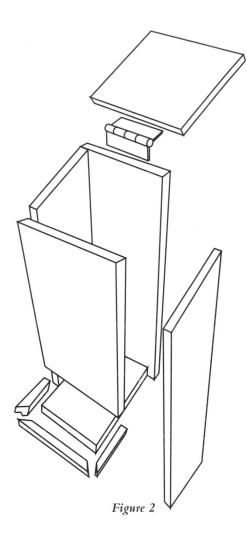

Figure 2

3. Using the ¹⁄₁₆ bit, drill four or five holes in the bottom for drainage. If you like, drill three holes in the front to allow for checking the feed level, using the ⁵⁄₆₄ bit.

4. Using the 4d nails, nail the front and back to the sides, sandwiching the sides between the front and back. See Figure 2.

5. Cut the bottom to fit; depending on the actual dimensions of your lumber, the bottom will need to be about 5⅞ or 6 inches wide. Fit the bottom into the sides and back, so that it's flush with the bottom of the feeder. (The bottom butts up against the back and projects out from the front to form a trough.)

6. Screw one side of the hinge to the center of the back, on the outside. Screw the other half of the hinge to the bottom of the lid, centering the hinge side to side and positioning it ½ inch from the edge.

7. Cut two pieces of face trim 3¼ inches long. Cut one piece 7½ inches long. Using the wire brads, nail the trim around the trough.

8. Paint or stain the feeder if desired.

9. With the ⁵⁄₆₄ bit, drill a pilot hole on each side for a screw eye. Center the holes about ¾ inch from the top. Insert the screw eyes and hold the feeder up to check the balance. Adjust the locations if necessary.

10. Tie the rope to the screw eyes, shortening it as desired. (Thirty inches for each side of the rope is a good length.)

NOTE: Metric equivalents are on page 128.

Contributing Designers

LOVEETA BAKER is a graphic artist and fabric designer.

LOU EREMITA is a silversmith and jewelry designer whose creations range from simple, hand-crafted silver hoops with beads to complex metalwork. He sells his work at craft fairs and shops.

RENEE GARCIA is a graphic designer who loves to cook. Herb-infused oils are the most recent (and most welcome) addition to her pantry.

DANA IRWIN is a painter, a graphic designer, and an art director for Lark Books in Asheville, North Carolina.

LAUREY MASTERTON is owner and head chef of Laurey's Catering in Asheville, North Carolina. She recently reissued (and wrote an introduction for) her mother's famous *Blueberry Hill Cookbook*.

JOSENA MCCAIG is a floral designer. Before starting her own business, she was a designer for the Biltmore Estate in Asheville, North Carolina.

ALYCE NADEAU grows 200 different herbs for her business, Goldenrod Mountain Herbs, in Deep Gap, North Carolina. She is the author of *Making and Selling Herbal Crafts* (Sterling Publishing, 1995).

BILL PARKER retired from teaching and promptly went to work as a full-time crafter, along with wife Nan. The Parkers, who specialize in angel figures, sell their work at craft fairs.

MARY PARKER pursues a career in public sector finance in order to indulge her passion for sewing, designing, and fabric in general.

CAROL PARKS is an author, editor, and seamstress. Her recent books include *The Complete Book of Window Treatments and Curtains* and *Make Your Own Great Vests* (both from Sterling Publishing).

JUDITH ROBERTSON is a community health researcher whose passions include chamber music, birdwatching, and sewing.

MAGGIE ROTMAN learned to love fabric and sewing during her school days in England. She incorporates stamping, painting, and other forms of surface design in her custom clothing.

CYNTHIA RUTLEDGE is a designer of bead jewelry who teaches beadwork to beginning and advanced students. Her work appears in a variety of publications and galleries.

PATTY AND MIMI SCHLEICHER (mother and daughter) are internationally known marblers of paper and fabric, but they also create other decorative papers, such as paste papers. They are coauthors of *Marbled Designs* (Lark Books, 1993).

SHEILA SCHULZ is a short-story writer, an avid reader, and a professional decorative painter.

TERRY TAYLOR is a former kindergarten teacher who tries his hand at absolutely every craft that comes along.

KIM TIBBALS is an art director and graphic designer who pours much of her artistic energy into drawing, sewing, herbal crafts, gardening, and broom making.

SHARON TOMPKINS is a decorative painter who works on everything from walls to flowerpots.

CINDY VANDEWART designs and makes beaded jewelry, which she sells at craft fairs.

VIRGINIA WAYNE is a designer of bead jewelry. Particularly fond of silver, copper, and brass wire, she constantly finds new ways to combine them with beads.

DIANE WEAVER is an artist, designer, herbalist, and author. Her most recent book is *Painted Furniture* (Sterling, 1995). The handsome, rocklike pot that holds the winter garden on page 8 was crafted by Dick Weaver.

CRAIG WEIS is a woodworker and builder who enjoys wind surfing.

BARBARA WRIGHT would rather string or wire beads than do just about anything else. She has taught hundreds of people the ins and outs of basic jewelry making.

ELLEN ZAHOREC is a mixed media studio artist who specializes in handmade paper and collage. Her work has been shown internationally and is part of numerous private and corporate collections.

Acknowledgements

Thanks to Julie Colando, who stamped the papers used as backgrounds on pages 58 and 102; to Josena McCaig, who added her own special touches to the book; and to Monroe Moore, for lending a hand with styling the food photos.

Project Index

METRIC EQUIVALENTS FOR WOOD PROJECTS

$\frac{1}{16}$"	1.5 mm	10"	25 cm
$\frac{1}{4}$"	6 mm	11"	28 cm
$\frac{1}{2}$"	1.5 cm	12"	30.5 cm
$\frac{3}{4}$"	2 cm	14"	35.5 cm
1"	2.5 cm	15"	38 cm
2"	5 cm	18"	45.5 cm
3"	7.5 cm	2 feet (24")	61 cm
4"	10 cm	3 feet (36")	.9 m
5"	12.5 cm	4 feet (48")	1.2 m
6"	15 cm	2 yards	1.8 m
7"	18 cm	8 feet	2.5 m
8"	20.5 cm		